SINGER

Sewing for Style

Cy DeCosse Incorporated
Minnetonka, Minnesota

SINGER

SEWING REFERENCE LIBRARY™

Sewing for Style

Contents

Library of Congress Cataloging in Publication Data

Sewing for Style

(Singer Sewing Reference Library)
Includes index.
1. Dressmaking. 2. Sewing.
I. Cy DeCosse Inc.
II. Singer Company Dept. of Sewing Education. III. Series.
TT515.S47   1985   646.4   85-13074
ISBN 0-86573-207-8
ISBN 0-86573-208-6 (pbk.)
Distributed by: Contemporary Books, Inc., Chicago, Illinois

CY DE COSSE INCORPORATED
Chairman: Cy DeCosse
President: James B. Maus
Executive Vice President: William B. Jones

SEWING FOR STYLE
Created by: The Editors of Cy DeCosse Incorporated, in cooperation with the Singer Education Department. Singer is a trademark of The Singer Company and is used under license.

Project Director: Gail Devens
Managing Editor: Reneé Dignan

Art Directors: James Olson, William Nelson, Susan Schultz
Editors: Susan Meyers, Bernice Maehren
Writer: Peggy Bendel
Sample Supervisor: Phyllis Galbraith
Sewing Staff: Bridget Haugh, Carol Neumann, Jeanine Boehmler, Lori Collins, Liz Hickerson, Rita Opseth, Mary Kay Rosch
Garment Construction: Sheila Duffy, Wendy Fedie, Carol Haw
Photographers: Kris Boom, Tony Kubat, Jerry Robb

Production Consultant: Christine Watkins
Production Manager: Jim Bindas
Asst. Production Manager: Julie Churchill
Production Staff: Michelle Alexander, Yelena Konrardy, Nancy Nardone, Jennie Smith, Bryan Trandem, Nik Wogstad
Consultants: LaVern Bell; Grace Chura; Wendy Fedie; Carol Haw; Louise Moline; Sherri Johnson; Gerry Robins; Zoe Graul; The Singer Company; Kris Mason; Jim Nelson, Homestyles; Becky Stevens, B. Blumenthal & Co., Inc.

Contributing Manufacturers: B. Blumenthal & Co., Inc.; Crown Textile Company; Stacy Fabrics Corp.; Pellon Corp.; EZ International; Uniquely You Dress Forms; Exotic Silks; Dyno Merchandise Corporation; baskets and shelving from Closet Maid by Clairson; The Singer Company
Color Separations: La Cromolito
Printing: R. R. Donnelley & Sons Co. (0786)

How to Use This Book

Sewing for Style goes beyond the beginner stage of sewing to the next level of expertise. With this book you can add to the basic skills gained from personal experience. Once you have mastered the basics, use *Sewing for Style* as a guide to more advanced sewing.

Although this book is not a beginning sewing book, neither is it just for experts. A little general sewing experience is all you need. Learning the basics may take only a short amount of time, but perfecting sewing techniques is a life-long pursuit for most of us. Those with some experience seek faster, more professional, and more creative construction techniques. No matter what level your skills have reached, there are always new fabrics, notions, tools, and patterns to explore.

To help you progress in your sewing, the book is divided into four sections that guide you in selection of materials, sewing techniques, shortcut tailoring, and creative details. Each section of the book builds on the information in the preceding sections. As you turn to a specific technique that you need, keep in mind that related information may be available as a reference in other parts of the book.

All four sections feature step-by-step instructions for quality dressmaking. A color photograph illustrates each step, showing you exactly how it is done. (Contrasting thread is sometimes used in the photographs so you can see the sewing techniques more clearly.) The instructions are not for entire projects but for individual techniques to use with any commercial pattern. The techniques were chosen to simplify sewing, save time, and result in more professional-looking garments.

A Guide to Quality & Style

The first section introduces a variety of fabrics, notions, and supplies, as well as tips for making expert selections. Because fusing offers a time-saving and successful method for interfacing, we have used fusible interfacings almost exclusively in the samples and sewing techniques. Learn about fusible interfacings and how to choose the right one for a specific sewing project. Developing good judgment about garment fit is also important to your sewing progress. This first section explains ease and the ways that fabrics and fashions influence fit.

As your commitment to sewing increases, your collection of sewing equipment naturally grows. When it is time to organize your tools and supplies, or to set up a permanent place for sewing, turn to the model room and adapt the features that are convenient for you.

Expert Techniques & Shortcuts

Professional dressmakers were our consultants for this book; the methods featured reflect their ways of handling details such as collars, cuffs, sleeves, shoulder pads, pockets, and waistbands. Some of the dressmakers' methods are shortcuts, and some are alternatives to basic techniques. All emphasize achieving high standards of workmanship without complicated and unnecessary work.

Easy, simplified tailoring methods using fusible interfacing are another focus of this book. You can learn these techniques in the step-by-step tailoring instructions. An important part of this contemporary tailoring approach is the way a project is organized. As you will see, all fusing is done at one time as the first step. The remaining steps fall into place logically and in record time. Included are techniques for tailoring a jacket, plus instructions for lining jackets, pants, and skirts.

A Source of Creative Ideas

Distinctive details are attractive, high-quality extras you can add to a commercial pattern. They include treatments for garment edges, unusual seams, and surface decorations.

None of these details requires extensive sewing or mysterious pattern drafting. In fact, few of these details require time-consuming handwork; most can be sewn by machine. All of them, however, are creative ways to satisfy the impulse to sew something special. Use our sampler of details as a source of ideas for creating your own designer touches to make your garments look like boutique originals.

Sewing for Style is dedicated to helping you acquire new skills and achieve the exact results you want from each sewing project. New skills lead to greater confidence in your abilities and the confidence to add your own personal style to your projects.

Sewing Expertise

Fabrics

The more you sew, the more flair you'll have for choosing fabrics. Before working with an unfamiliar fabric, practice stitching, pressing, and other techniques to find the best methods to use.

Fabrics vary in fiber content, type of weave or knit, weight, and surface texture. Beyond these structural differences, there are differences in the fashion elements of color, print or pattern, and *hand* — how the fabric feels, the way it drapes, whether it tends to wrinkle and ravel, whether it is soft or stiff, and whether it stretches or is stable. With practice, thinking about these points comes naturally whenever you examine a bolt of fabric.

Drape the fabric over your body in front of a full-length mirror. Use the illustrations on the front of the pattern envelope, and the suggested fabric types listed on the back, to guide your selection. Also be confident enough to use your own ideas. One of the rewards of sewing is creating one-of-a-kind clothing that expresses your personal taste.

Choosing Quality in Fabrics

When you invest time and workmanship in a sewing project, a quality fabric makes your efforts worthwhile. Choose fabrics like those used in expensive ready-to-wear garments. These fabrics do justice to more advanced sewing skills.

Fibers give fabrics distinction and character. Fabrics made entirely or primarily from natural fibers — wool, silk, cotton, and linen — respond beautifully to stitching and pressing. Many fabrics made from synthetic fibers, such as polyester or acrylic, copy the fashion effect of natural fibers but have advantages such as wrinkle resistance and easy care.

Another mark of quality is fabric weave. Hold the fabric up to light to check whether the weave is fine and even. Check that the fabric is *on-grain*, with lengthwise and crosswise threads at right angles throughout. Fabric must be on-grain for a garment to fit and drape correctly. On knits the ribs should look straight and not curve toward the edges.

Examine the fabric completely before you buy. If the fabric has been folded onto a bolt, check the crease, where excess color often rubs off. If the crease looks faded, reject the fabric. Sometimes uneven color shows at the selvages, too. Fiber content affects color stability. Cotton, wool, and acrylic have a good affinity for dyes, so fabrics from these fibers are less likely to fade. Because pure linen fibers do not dye well, linen fabrics are often left in the natural beige color of the fiber. Silk dyes well but may bleed and fade when washed.

Lightweight fabrics such as (1) crepe de chine, (2) charmeuse, and (3) tissue faille drape softly. Use (4) jacquard weaves for softly styled garments. Shirtings such as (5) oxford cloth, (6) chambray, (7) batiste, and (8) handkerchief linen are classics. On (9) jersey knit the ribs run lengthwise on the right side. Use (10) challis for softly draped styles.

Mediumweight fabrics such as **(1)** wool flannel, **(2)** herringbone tweed, **(3)** silk linen, **(4)** raw silk, **(5)** silk noil, **(6)** homespun, **(7)** double knit, and **(8)** linen-likes are excellent choices for tailored jackets and other separates. Firmer fabrics such as **(9)** gabardine and **(10)** poplin are suitable for garments with simple seams and crisp details.

Heavyweight or bulky fabrics such as **(1)** Harris tweed, **(2)** brushed mohair, and **(3)** open weaves look best when sewn in simple pattern styles. For coats and jackets, choose **(4)** melton, **(5)** fleece, **(6)** camel's hair, and **(7)** wide-wale corduroy. These fabrics may also be tailored without interfacings or linings for loose-fitting capes and coats.

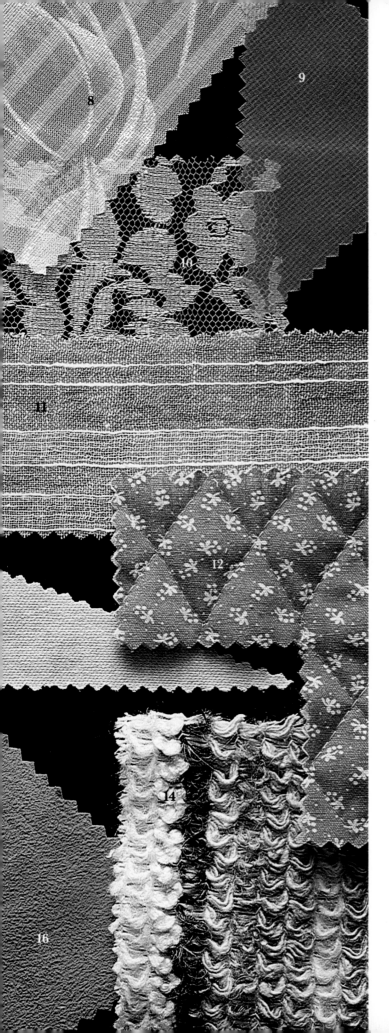

Handling Specialty Fabrics

Some specialty fabrics are actually easier to sew than many traditional fabrics; others may need an extra sewing step or extra care.

Napped fabrics such as (1) corduroy and (2) velvet have a fluffy, soft, or hairy surface texture on the right side. If you stroke these fabrics lengthwise, the direction in which the surface feels smoother is *with the nap*. The other direction is *against the nap*. The color probably looks darker against the nap and frosted with the nap. Because the surface has this one-way quality, pin patterns on these fabrics using a "with nap" layout, one which has all the pattern pieces headed in the same direction. The back of the pattern envelope tells you if this layout requires additional fabric.

Lustrous fabrics such as (3) brocade, (4) fabrics with metallic fibers, (5) satin, and (6) damask also require a "with nap" pattern layout. Cutting all the garment sections in one direction guarantees uniform color shading in the finished garment. Also in this category are (7) silk and silk-type fabrics, which have a slight surface sheen. Some lustrous fabrics must be pressed with low heat and a dry iron to avoid water spots or other damage. Save scraps to test pressing techniques, and use a press cloth to protect the fabric.

Sheer transparencies such as (8) voile, (9) chiffon, (10) lace, and (11) gauze look best with narrow seams and require edge finishes because all inside construction is visible from the outside of the garment. Overlocked seams and edges are ideal for these fabrics. To match the delicate nature of sheers, use extra-fine thread and a size 9/65 needle for machine stitching.

Novel fabrics may require a "with nap" pattern layout. To make a reversible garment, use (12) quilted fabric, which has two right sides. Use flat-fell seams, which look finished from both sides, and binding or fold-over braid to finish hems and front closings. Sew (13) lightweight knits with any narrow seam; (14) bulky sweater knits require nonbulky overlocked seams. For a true sweater look, finish waist, cuffs, and neckline with color-matched ribbing trim. Fabrics such as (15) leather and (16) heavyweight synthetic suede require unique seams and hems. Ordinary seams may be too bulky. Easy lapped seams work well because the raw edges do not ravel. Face hems with a separate fabric strip; or neatly trim the edge, and topstitch.

Buttons

The assortment of buttons available varies in style, size, and color, depending on trends in fashion and fabrics. There are also enduring button classics.

Fashion buttons are often made from casein (a plastic) or synthetic materials such as nylon, acetate, or polyester/acrylic. Casual **(1)** colored buttons, **(2)** novelty buttons, and **(3)** two-tone buttons come from these sources. Fashion styles for formal wear may have **(4)** rhinestones or imitation jewels; formal styles also include **(5)** pearl-like buttons, sometimes trimmed in gold.

Classic styles from natural materials include **(6)** pearl shirt buttons and **(7)** ocean pearl buttons with a natural off-white or soft gray coloring that is a universal neutral. Buttons from other natural materials such as **(8)** horn, **(9)** leather, **(10)** wood, and **(11)** glass have distinctive colors and textures. Classic **(12)** gold and silvertone blazer sets have a shank and come in two sizes; the smaller size is a standard decoration for sleeve vents. Other metal buttons include **(13)** bronze and copper-colored buttons without shanks.

Tips for Selecting Buttons

Select buttons as carefully as you select jewelry to complement a garment. Choose color-matched buttons when you want to make a buttoned closing less conspicuous. If the garment is styled in a soft, feminine manner, choose delicate buttons. Tailored jackets suggest a functional, simple button style.

Button size can be up to ⅛" (3 mm) larger or smaller than that recommended by your pattern, but it is best to find the size suggested. Changing the button size may mean respacing buttonholes and running the risk of choosing buttons too bold or too dainty in scale.

Button styles range from plain to elaborate. Generally, the more buttons on a garment, the plainer the style should be. Use unusual, highly decorative buttons sparingly for a dramatic but uncluttered effect.

Button weight should relate to the garment fabric. Select a lightweight button for lightweight fabrics. On bulky or textured fabrics, find buttons that look thick or heavy, even though they may weigh little.

Care of buttons should be compatible with the garment. Most buttons can be washed or drycleaned, but some require special care. Wood buttons must be drycleaned, for example, because they swell in water. Crystal buttons can crack if touched by an iron. Jeweled buttons should be removed before a garment is cleaned.

Trims

Purchased trims can give the impression of skillful, detailed sewing on a garment, even though applying trim takes little time. Add a **(1)** heraldic emblem to a blazer pocket, for example, for an authentic, classic touch. Ready-made **(2)** novelty appliqués add whimsy and the look of hand embroidery to children's clothes. For adult casual wear, there are **(3)** sports motifs in appliqué form.

Appliqués can be added to a garment at any time; other trims should be added during construction. Band trims, such as **(4)** satin, **(5)** embroidered ribbon, **(6)** velvet, **(7)** grosgrain, **(8)** plaited flat braid, and **(9)** narrow soutache braid, are easier to apply to flat garment sections before sewing side seams. Elaborate, fancy band trims are often called

(10) passementerie braids. Narrow trimmings, such as **(11)** piping, **(12)** cording, and **(13)** fagoting, are sewn into seams.

Lace trims come in many forms. Use as band trims **(14)** lace beading with openings to weave ribbon through and **(15)** galloon lace, which is bordered on two edges. Apply **(16)** lace medallions in the same way that you apply appliqués. As seam insertions, use **(17)** lace edging, which is bordered on one edge, and **(18)** ruffled lace edging.

Glittering trims include band trims that are **(19)** beaded, **(20)** sequined, **(21)** metallic, and **(22)** jeweled. Sportier trims include **(23)** leather piping and **(24)** leather-type banding. Trims such as **(25)** loose beads, **(26)** individual sequins, and **(27)** sequined appliqués are sewn to a garment by hand. Elegant trims such as **(28)** fur collars and **(29)** feathers make luxurious details.

Tips for Choosing Trims

A contrast in color between trim and garment fabric is often more effective than striving for a perfect match. However, some fabric manufacturers offer ruffles and bindings or color-coordinated trims that are dyed to match for a custom-made look.

Trim weight can be deceptive. Consider how many rows of braid or ruffled lace you will use, for example, and avoid overloading the fabric with a treatment so heavy it interferes with garment drape. Use only lightweight trims on lightweight fabrics. Many beaded and jeweled trims are heavy; apply them to firm fabrics, or back the fabric with interfacing in trimmed areas.

Broaden your choice of trims by shopping in home decorating departments and upholstery supply stores. Home furnishing trims have rich textures that complement many bulky, heavyweight, and deeply textured garment fabrics.

Care requirements of trims should be compatible with those of the garment. Many home furnishing trims must be drycleaned, but most dressmaking trims can be washed. Beaded, sequined, and jeweled trims may require special care. Appliqués using these materials can be removed before the garment is cleaned, solving care problems.

Plan trim placement for pleasing balance and proportion. For example, repeat a hemline trim somewhere else on the garment, such as at collar and cuffs, for a harmonious design. Select a small-scale trim for a small garment or delicate fabric. Avoid placing band trims across the fullest areas of your figure or positioning appliqués at the bust.

Interfacings

Interfacings are used inside a garment to shape, strengthen, support, or stiffen the fashion fabric. In dressmaking, portions of a garment (such as the collar, cuffs, and waistband) are interfaced. In tailoring, entire garment sections (such as the jacket front and sleeves) as well as details (such as pockets and vents) are interfaced.

Patterns usually suggest interfacing a garment where it is necessary. You may prefer to apply interfacings in additional places to improve the workmanship in your garment or to improve the performance of a fashion fabric. Designers often use several types of interfacings within a garment, each with a different degree of crispness. It's a practice worth following to achieve professional results from interfacings.

Fabrics made especially for use as interfacings are available in fusible and nonfusible forms. Fusible interfacings have been coated on one side with a heat-sensitive adhesive so the interfacing can be bonded to the fashion fabric with an iron. Occasionally a nonfusible interfacing is more appropriate for your fabric. It must be sewn to the fashion fabric by hand or machine.

Sheer nonwoven interfacings are the lightest in weight. Use them for delicate and semitransparent fabrics. There is a choice of colors, including a neutral skin tone, to blend with fabric colors or prints without showing through to the right side of the garment.

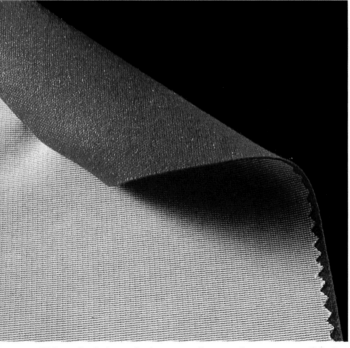

Tricot knit interfacings can be used on woven fabrics as well as on knits. They are often used to back entire garment sections to add body and wrinkle resistance. Tricot can be used in areas of detail, too. It remains soft after fusing and does not change the way the fashion fabric drapes.

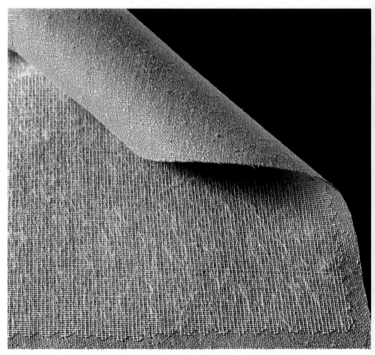

Weft insertion interfacings are stable lengthwise, but can stretch and recover crosswise. Use them on light to mediumweight fabrics and for a soft, natural look when tailoring. Cut weft insertion interfacing on the lengthwise grain to stabilize details on garments; cut crosswise for supple shaping.

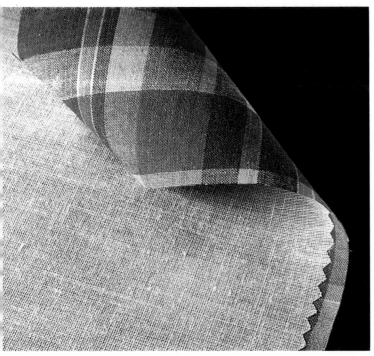

Woven interfacings have a lengthwise and crosswise grain that corresponds to a woven fashion fabric. For stability they are generally cut on the same grain as the area to be interfaced; however, cutting them on the bias will add softer, more supple shaping.

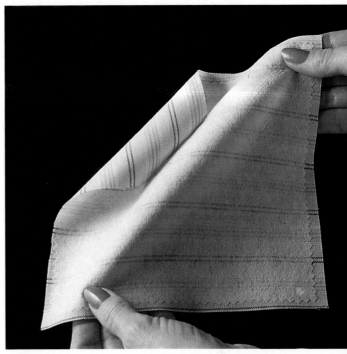

All-bias nonwoven interfacings give in all directions and can be cut without concern for grain. Several weights are available with soft or crisp finishes. Also available are stretch nonwovens, which have a great degree of crosswise stretchability. Knits stretch even after the interfacing has been fused in place.

Hair canvas is a woven fusible used on medium to heavyweight fabrics. It is a standard tailoring interfacing. Hair canvas is firm and resilient, and gives garments a crisp, structured shape.

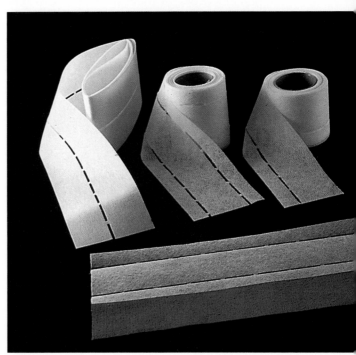

Precut nonwoven interfacings save sewing time on straight details such as waistbands, shirt cuffs, front placket openings, and jacket hems. Match perforated openings of precut interfacings with garment seamlines and foldlines to eliminate bulk.

Using Fusible Interfacings

The only sure way to predict how a fusible interfacing will perform is to test-fuse a sample to a scrap of the fashion fabric you are using. Keep a variety of fusible interfacings on hand. Then you can try out several interfacings before you begin a sewing project. Stockpiled fusibles do not go to waste. Sooner or later, each will fulfill a purpose in one of your sewing projects.

Fusibles become firmer after fusing, but how firm they will become is impossible to know without a test. Another variable is color; after fusing, some colored interfacings darken. A test shows exactly what effect the interfacing has on a fabric after bonding. Once you know this, you can determine whether you have selected the right fusible interfacing for the fabric and pattern style.

Check the permanence of the fused bond. When fused correctly, interfacing appears blended into the fabric weave. You should not be able to peel back edges of interfacing. There should be no bubbles or unfused areas. No shiny adhesive should be visible between the interfacing and jacket fabric. Correct mistakes by re-fusing. Or steam interfacing to peel it off; cut a new interfacing and fuse again.

Tips for Buying Fusible Interfacings

Read the interfacing bolt label or the plastic wrapper to find the manufacturer's recommendations for use. Fabric types and garment styles mentioned can help you make a preliminary choice. Some fusible interfacings are available especially for tailoring jackets or for crisp details, for example. Others have low-melt adhesives for delicate fabrics or a structure that stretches with knits.

Choose interfacing weight by fabric weight. Interfacing may be crisper than the fashion fabric, but it should never be heavier. Be aware that after fusing, the fabric and bonded interfacing will seem a little heavier than before fusing. Fusible interfacings come in a range of weights from very lightweight sheers to heavy craft weights, so you can select those that are suitable for your purpose.

Determine whether interfaced garment areas should be soft, like the front closing on a silky blouse, or crisp, like shirt collars and cuffs. Practically every fusible interfacing is labeled either "soft" or "crisp" to describe the results you can expect. Soft interfacings add body to fabrics. Crisp interfacings stiffen fabrics.

Layer fabric over interfacing to select the best interfacing color. Many interfacings come in a choice of white, black, gray, and beige, and some come in other colors, such as red and blue. The color of the interfacing should not show through or change the color of the fashion fabric.

How to Test Fusible Interfacings

1) Fuse interfacing to fabric, following manufacturer's directions precisely. Time, heat, moisture, and pressure can vary. Test should reflect actual fusing conditions you will use on garment.

2) Use scrap of fashion fabric at least 6" (15 cm) square. Use smaller piece of fusible interfacing about 4" (10 cm) square. Try several different interfacings to compare results.

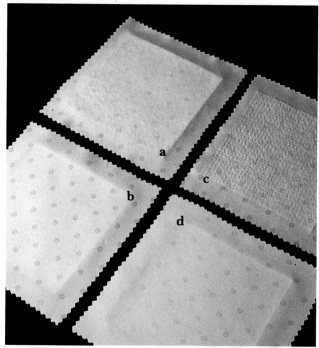

3) Allow fused sample to cool completely. Turn sample to right side and see if interfacing shows through as visible ridge **(a)**, if interfacing has changed fabric color **(b)**, or if fabric has been damaged by heat and moisture **(c)**. If any of these conditions exist, select another fusible interfacing. Sample **(d)** has proper appearance after fusing.

4) Judge the difference in drape between interfaced and non-interfaced fabric **(a)**. There should be no great contrast in crispness; this would make garment unattractive and uncomfortable. In sample **(b)**, interfacing is too soft for fabric and feels limp. Sample **(c)** shows good relationship between fabric and interfacing. In **(d)**, interfacing is too crisp for fabric and feels stiff.

A Place to Sew

Sewing is more enjoyable and much easier when you have a permanent place to sew with everything close at hand. Whether you can dedicate a large or small space to sewing, use it wisely by organizing your collection of equipment and supplies.

An efficient way to organize is according to sewing task. Sewing involves three major activities: layout/cutting, stitching, and pressing. Therefore it is practical to arrange three work stations in your sewing area similar to the work triangle kitchen planners use to locate range, sink, and refrigerator. Assemble all the equipment and supplies that relate specifically to each sewing activity, and keep them handy to the area where they will be used.

You also need storage space. Sewing naturally encourages a stockpile of fabrics, trims, interfacings, notions, and patterns earmarked for future sewing projects. Storage hardware and modular units, like those used for kitchens and closets, work well in a sewing area. Plastic-coated wall shelves, for example, keep supplies out of the way but within reach. Select components suitable to the size of your sewing space. Allow room for hanging garments and projects in progress; the edge of open shelving can provide a hanging surface. Hang folded fabric over padded suit hangers, or place in drawers.

Use wall-mounted racks and hooks for small items such as scissors, lint brush, and rolls of tape. A hanging thread rack keeps thread upright and visible. Other small items can be stored in a sportsman's tackle box with stepped trays or a utility box with clear plastic drawers.

A sewing machine should have ample flat work surface around it to support the fabric. An office chair rolls easily between machines and other work areas, and it adjusts for your height and comfort.

Organizing a Sewing Area

Layout/cutting area. A padded work surface, made from plywood or a hollow door, is large enough for laying fabric flat. Square corners aid in straightening grainlines; a muslin covering prevents the fabric from sliding. You can also pin into the work surface and use it as a pressing table for large projects. A magnetic pin cushion grabs pins for faster cleanup. A handy basket with hooks holds shears and other cutting aids.

Stitching area. Store machine attachments, presser feet, replacement needles, instruction manual, and maintenance tools nearby. If you have an overlock machine, keep it next to your conventional machine. Both should be ready to use when you're working on a sewing project. A bulletin board can hold the pattern guide sheet for ready reference. Keep thread near the machines.

Pressing area. A tabletop ironing board can be placed near the sewing machines or on a padded work surface; large pieces of fabric will not stretch out or drag on the floor. Steam/spray iron, hand steamer, and pressing tools (such as tailor's ham, sleeve board, point presser/clapper, seam roll, and press cloths) can be stored within arm's reach. A well-organized pressing station encourages the good habit of pressing as you sew.

Storage. Group similar items such as buttons, trims, zippers, and threads; put each group in see-through containers so you can see at once what you have and where it is. Cover fabric with sheeting or acid-free tissue paper, not plastic, to store on a long-term basis. Roll fusible interfacings on cardboard tubes for storage without wrinkling.

Overlock Machines

If you set up your sewing area with a conventional sewing machine and an overlock machine side by side, you can draw upon the strengths of both machines for sewing projects. Overlock sewing machines, also called *merrow* sewing machines or *sergers,* are special-purpose machines. A set of cutting blades, located in front of the needle, trims the raw fabric edges just before they are sewn. The machine automatically overcasts the just-trimmed raw edges as the fabric passes under the needle. With an overlock machine your garment will look professionally sewn because overlock machines are used by fashion designers and industrial garment manufacturers. Overlock machines are timesavers because they perform three steps at once — trimming, stitching, and overcasting.

Overlock machines produce basic overlock and chainstitch formations for use on seams, hems, and edges. The photos, opposite, show only a few of the many capabilities of the machines. The machines excel at making narrow, edge-finished seams on a broad range of fabrics, even problem fabrics. Fabrics that ravel, such as corduroy, denim, and linen weaves, as well as bulky fabrics, such as heavy sweater knits, are easy to sew on an overlock machine. So are slippery blouse and lining fabrics, and lightweight sheers, such as lingerie knits and chiffon. Make overlocked seams whenever you desire a narrow seam that is pressed to one side. First, however, be sure the garment fits. Once the seam allowances have been trimmed and overlocked, there is no room left for making alterations if the garment is too small.

If you prefer to make a plain, pressed-open seam, you can use an overlock machine just to finish the raw edges. Run the garment section through the machine either before or after sewing the seam to overcast the raw edges.

Overlock machines can also be used for hems. One type of overlocked hem is a narrow, rolled hem that is thread-bound. This hem is often used for blouses, formal gowns, table napkins, scarves, and lingerie. The other type is a blind hem, often used on jeans and other sportswear.

Two Types of Overlock Machines

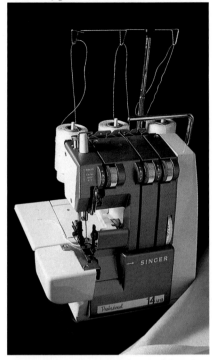

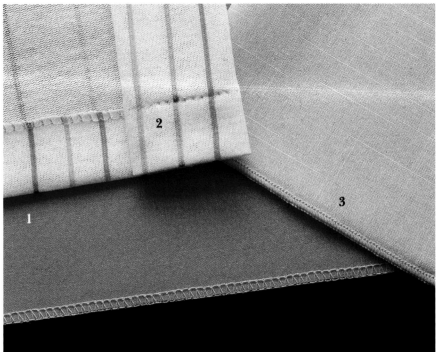

Three-thread overlock machine is versatile for fashion sewing. Economical cones hold 1,000 yd. (950 m) or more of thread and are practical because overlock machine uses a great amount of thread.

Example of typical three-thread seam **(1)** shows interlocking loops of thread, which distinguish overlocked from conventionally overcast seams. Fold fabric to overlock blind hem **(2)** from inside of garment. Adjust tension settings to make narrow hem **(3)** quickly on many kinds of fabrics. Both blind hem and narrow hem are exceptionally sturdy.

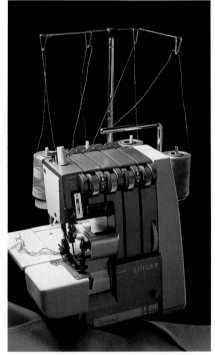

Four-thread overlock machine uses four threads and two needles. With removal of one needle, it converts to two-thread overlocking.

Example of typical four-thread seam **(1)** shows how overedged seam is reinforced by separate chainstitched seam. This stitch is called a *safety stitch*. Remove one machine needle for two-thread overedging **(2)**. Remove one needle and disengage cutting blades for chainstitching **(3)**; chainstitches are easy to remove and can be used for basting.

Fitting

Sewing offers the opportunity to create fashions that custom-fit your figure. A well-fitted garment is smooth without pulls and wrinkles that indicate too tight or too loose areas. Sleeves are the correct length, the waist is just snug enough, and pleats fall to the hem without sinking inward or spreading out. You can move with comfort, whether sitting, reaching, bending, or stretching, and you will not strain seams to the breaking point.

Factors That Influence Fit

The most basic element in fitting is having the right pattern size. To eliminate many fitting problems, use your body measurements to select pattern size. Those measurements include high bust, bust, waist, hips, back waist length, and height. Also, use the pattern appropriate to your figure type. If you are petite, for example, you can avoid most fitting headaches if you work with a Miss Petite size pattern rather than a Miss.

Fashion styles vary in the way they fit the body. Fit is part of the design. Some styles follow the figure closely, others are full cut and barely echo the figure at all, and there are fitting variations in between. Patterns for coats and jackets are sized to fit over other garments. If the pattern shows a coat worn over a jacket worn over a blouse, the three items will have a graduated fit for comfort.

Finally, your choice of fabric makes a difference in the way a garment fits. A pattern sewn in a soft jersey knit will fit in a completely different way from the same pattern sewn in a crisp taffeta. Some patterns require stretch knits or two-way stretch knits because the garment fit takes advantage of fabric elasticity. If you satisfy the pattern's fabric requirements, your garment will fit the way it should.

Fitting As You Sew

You must make any basic changes in length on the pattern pieces before cutting out fabric sections; however, many improvements in fit can be made during construction. Try on your garment after sewing the major front, back, side, and shoulder seams. Pin any shoulder pads in place. Check the fit while wearing the undergarments and accessories, such as belt and shoes, you plan to wear with the

finished garment. Taking in or letting out seams at this point in the sewing is easy.

While sewing progresses, try on the garment for fit as many times as needed. For example, it's a good idea to test the fit after sewing in one sleeve. Make sure ease at the sleeve cap is distributed to fit your figure, and check sleeve length. Then you can sew the other sleeve with confidence that it will fit.

Tips for Fitting As You Sew

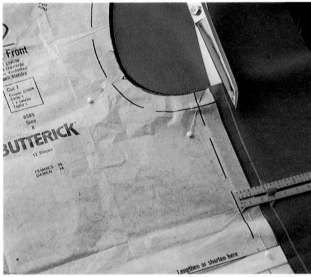

Allow 1" (2.5 cm) seams at sides of garment if you think changes in fit will be necessary. Seams can be let out to add as much as 2" (5 cm) around garment if needed. If extra allowance is not needed, trim seam to standard width after fitting.

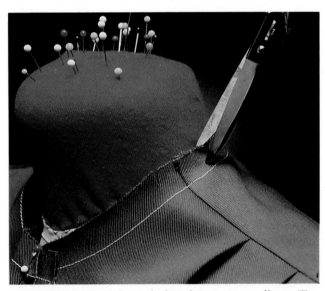

Staystitch neck and armhole edges on seamlines. Try on garment, right side out. Clip up to ¼" (6 mm) from staystitching until neck seamlines fall in proper position on figure.

Mark alterations on outside of garment with pins, or use thread to baste-mark delicate fabrics.

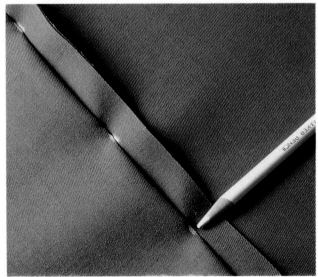

Use chalk or marking pen to transfer changes to inside of garment by tracing pinned or basted folds. Traced lines are new stitching lines for seams.

Judging Fit

Be particular about how your garments fit. Fitting as you sew takes a little extra time, but keep at it until you are satisfied. You will quickly learn which fitting changes you need consistently; then you can save time by making them early in a project.

Recognizing fitting problems is not always easy because we often see what we want to see when we look at ourselves in a mirror. Checking your own view from the back is physically awkward, so if possible ask someone to help you fit your garments. Determine the source of any fitting problems and resolve to fix them.

Apply the fitting standards described on these two pages to judge how well garments fit. Stand normally to study seam alignment. In general, vertical seams should fall straight to the floor, and horizontal seams should be parallel to the floor. Look carefully to be sure there are no wrinkles. In addition, move around to judge how the garment feels. Walk, sit down, reach forward, and reach up to spot any poorly fitted areas. A well-fitted garment allows you to move freely and returns to its original position when you are stationary.

Armhole seams should look smooth and feel comfortable. On classic set-in sleeve, ease around sleeve cap should have no wrinkles or puckers. Sleeve cap can be rotated toward back or front for better fit and distribution of ease. If armhole seams feel tight and stressed in back, open seams up and restitch to add width across back. Use a narrower seam allowance on the bodice only.

Shoulder seams should stop at end of shoulders for classic set-in sleeves. On raglan, kimono, and dolman sleeves, shaped shoulder seams or darts should match your shoulder contours. Extended shoulder seams, a fashion detail, require shoulder pads for good fit. Dropped shoulder seams, another fashion detail, rest on upper arms; check pattern shoulder markings to see how far below the shoulders the dropped seams belong.

Bust shaping should fall at fullest part of your bustline. If there are darts, they should end ½" to 1" (1.3 to 2.5 cm) short of your bust point. For a shirtwaist style, position one buttonhole at fullest part of your bustline; space other buttonholes evenly.

Waistline, waistband, or waist shaping should fall at natural waist. Bend sideways to find your natural waistline. Skirt or pants waistband has enough ease, from ½" to 1" (1.3 to 2.5 cm), for your thumb to fit comfortably between waistband and your abdomen.

Neckline or collar seams should rest on collarbone. If there is gaping, neckline is too big. If there is strain and wrinkling, neckline is too small and high for your bone structure; make seam deeper so neckline is in proper position.

Long sleeves, whether finished with cuffs or hems, should end at the wrist. Sleeves should be long enough so you can bend your elbow without straining garment. Full, gathered sleeves should blouse gracefully. Fitted sleeves often have darts or easing at elbow; be sure this extra shaping falls at the right place.

Side seams should fall in a direct line from underarm seams. If seams pull toward the front, garment front needs additional room to cover abdominal contours. If seams pull toward the back, garment back needs extra girth. There should be 2" to 4" (5 to 10 cm) of ease at hipline.

Hemline should be even distance from floor all around. Make sure hem is in flattering place for your height. Experiment to find best location, raising and lowering hemline with pins. Avoid placing the hem across the fullest part of your calves.

Understanding Ease

Ease is extra room that has been designed into a pattern for two reasons — for comfort and for design. Ease ensures that the garment sewn from the pattern is larger than your figure. You can measure the ease in a pattern at key points. Subtract the standard body measurements for your size (given on the back of the pattern envelope) from the measurements of the pattern pieces at bust, waist, hips, and back waist length; exclude seam allowances, darts, self-facings, and similar details as you measure. The difference between the two numbers is the ease allowance.

Amount of Ease

The amount of ease designed into a pattern varies from style to style. Fashion trends often dictate the amount of ease. Some silhouettes fit the body closely; other fashions may feature a looser look or a floating, oversized fit. The amount of ease differs with the type of garment, too.

Sometimes the ease is purely functional. The crotch seam of a jumpsuit has more ease than a pants crotch seam because the one-piece garment requires more room when you sit down. Jackets must have enough ease to fit over a sweater or blouse. Strapless bodices have little or no ease so that they hug the figure without slipping down. The pattern pieces for swimsuits can be smaller than the body measurements, a kind of negative ease; the highly elastic two-way stretch knit fabric used for swimsuits must be draped tightly to fit well when wet.

Fabrics & Ease

Fabric influences the amount of ease in a pattern. If the pattern specifies heavy coatings, for example, the thickness of the fabric has been taken into account and enough ease has been added for the pattern to fit well. Patterns for pleated skirts usually suggest thin, smooth fabrics when pleats fold into four layers of fabric at the waist and hips. Extra room is included in the pattern to accommodate these folded layers so the skirt fits smoothly.

At times you may select a fabric that requires an adjustment in the ease. Loosely woven fabrics should not be fitted closely, for example, and neither should leather, clinging jerseys, or fragile fabrics such as lace. Too close a fit stresses these fabrics and weakens seams. Allow extra-wide seam allowances, as described on page 27, and let out seams to add ease, if necessary, as you sew.

Preserving Ease

To help you predict how much ease is included in a pattern, pattern companies provide a description on the back of the pattern envelope. Phrases such as "close fitting," "semi-fitted," and "very loose fitting" suggest the way the garment should drape on your body. These clues help you avoid fitting loose styles too closely or letting the seams out too much on fitted styles. You should adjust the garment to fit your figure, keeping in mind the amount of ease the pattern furnishes.

To preserve the ease in a pattern, compare your figure measurements to the standard body measurements for your size. Any differences, plus or minus, indicate how much change to make when fitting the garment. For example, if your hips are 1" (2.5 cm) larger than the standard hip measurement, let out each side seam ¼" (6 mm) to add a total of 1" (2.5 cm). You have enlarged the garment to fit your figure without changing the amount of ease provided by the pattern.

Three Types of Fit

Fitted sheath has closely fitted silhouette with minimal ease. Darts shape garment to reveal figure at bust, waist, and hips. Amount of **ease at bust** varies from none to about 3" (7.5 cm). Avoid tendency to fit too closely; preserve enough ease so garment is comfortable.

Semi-fitted shirtdress is shaped to follow figure outline but skims figure. Waist may not be defined but may be suggested by contoured side seams. Amount of ease at bust ranges from about 4" to 5" (10 to 12.5 cm). This fit generally flatters full figures.

Loosely fitted dress has deep armholes and dropped shoulders; waistline is not defined. Amount of bust ease is generous, sometimes 8" (20.5 cm) or more. Presence of gathers or bloused waistline also signals loose fit. In general, loose fit is attractive on slender figures.

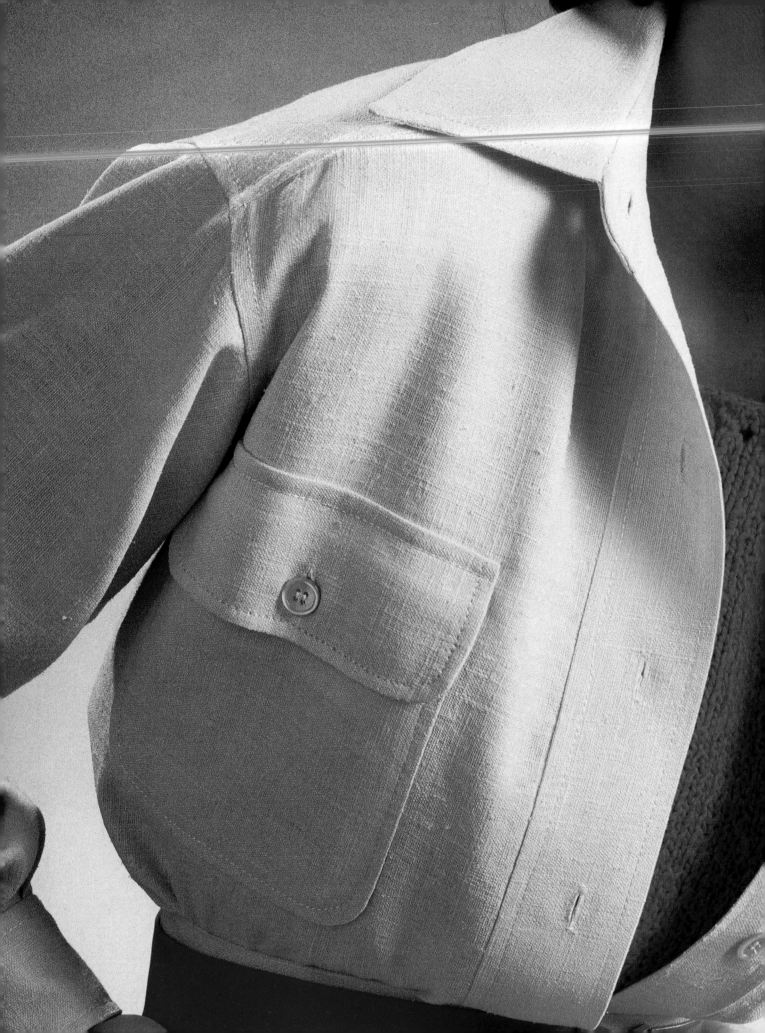

Wardrobe Planning

With contemporary sewing techniques you can expand your sewing abilities to include garments with more detailing and shaping. Being able to sew different types of collars, sleeves, and pockets, for example, adds variety to your projects and to your wardrobe. The more techniques you master, the more carefully you'll want to plan each sewing project so that everything you make fits into a well-coordinated wardrobe.

Before each season of the year, take the time to think about your sewing plans. Check your wardrobe and decide what items you would like to add. To get true value from a sewing plan, collect patterns and fabrics that can be worn with items you already own.

Sewing separate items as mix-and-match ensembles is a wise approach. This makes it possible to create many different outfits from a few, well-selected pieces. It enables you to build a wardrobe that is ready for any occasion. Sew the important items, such as jackets, pants, and skirts, from versatile neutral colors. To add sparkle, sew the smaller items, such as blouses, from bright colors and prints. With assorted belts, jewelry, shoes, and other accessories, you can change the look and mood of any ensemble.

You will enjoy sewing more and make fewer mistakes if you are not under pressure to finish quickly. Allow enough time to collect notions, assemble supplies, clean and oil your sewing machine, and sew at a leisurely, steady pace.

To gain the maximum benefits from your sewing, use these tips to form a plan before each season.

Distinguish between fashion fads and classics. Fads look new and can be an instant tonic for a tired wardrobe. Classics look familiar because they survive changing fashion trends. The cardigan jacket, pleat-front pants, shirtdress, and tailored blazer are some examples of timeless classics. Base your wardrobe on classics. Save fads for impulse sewing or minor items; fads go out of style quickly.

Sew classic styles in classic fabrics for maximum wear. Linen weaves, wool tweeds, gabardine, challis, crepe de chine, jersey, corduroy, double knits, and fine shirtings are fabrics that enjoy a long fashion life. Spend most of your sewing budget on fabrics like these, because you will wear the items for more seasons than fad items.

Shop with swatches from items in your wardrobe to select fabrics for your sewing plan. Few of us have an accurate color memory, and fabric samples prevent mistakes. For the best color coordination, check fabrics under indoor and outdoor lighting; examine fabrics up close and at a distance. Some fabric manufacturers design groups of complementary weaves, prints, and solid colors that you can use in any combination. This makes it easy for you to sew mix-and-match separates.

Techniques for Seams & Edges

Seam and Edge Finishes

Quality in sewing shows on the inside of a garment as well as on the outside. One sign of expertise is finishing raw fabric edges that show at seams, hems, and facings. Another is using special seams to control fraying, minimize bulk, or add strength. Edge finishes and special seams not only make a garment look neat and attractive on the inside, but they also make the garment last longer.

When you know how to sew different kinds of edges and seams, you can vary sewing methods according to the fabric in use. Consider whether the fabric is knit or woven. The weight of a fabric, its strength, and its tendency to ravel may also affect your choice of seams and seam finishes. Consider, too, the use and style of the garment — whether it will receive heavy wear and whether topstitching is suitable as a decorative accent.

The simplest technique is either to straight-stitch or to pink the edge. These two techniques are often combined for a flat finish. The techniques shown here are useful time after time. They form a working repertoire of skills for a wide range of fabrics.

Bound edges suit heavy and mediumweight fabrics. Use sheer tricot binding to encase raw edges. Use bias lining strips for the Hong Kong style binding. Binding is an excellent treatment for fabrics that ravel easily and for unlined jackets.

Special Seams

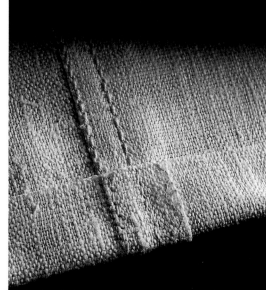

French seam encases both raw edges and looks like a narrow tuck on the inside. It's the traditional choice for sheer fabrics. Use a narrower seam for curved areas. French seams are stitched twice: first on the right side, then on the wrong side. The seam is strong even though it looks delicate.

Flat-fell seam hides both raw edges with sturdy, reversible stitching. First, the underneath seam allowance is trimmed. Then the top seam allowance is folded and edgestitched over trimmed edge. Flat-fell seams are used for durable jeans, active sportswear, and reversible garments.

Mock flat-fell seam looks like a flat-fell seam on the outside, but has an exposed seam allowance on the inside. After one seam allowance is trimmed, the other seam allowance is topstitched over it. Then the seam itself is edgestitched. Use only on fabrics that do not ravel.

Turned and stitched edges work best on lightweight woven fabrics. On heavier weights the folded edges are too bulky and can show on the right side of the garment. Another name for this method is *clean finishing*.

Zigzagged edges can be made with three-step or regular method. Zigzagging over the raw fabric edge works well on most fabrics, although the stitches can make a ridge on delicate fabrics. On knits, use an overedge stretch stitch.

Overlocked edges can be made on any fabric with an overlock machine, or serger. The machine trims and overcasts the fabric edge at the same time (page 25). Edges may be finished either before or after sewing plain seams.

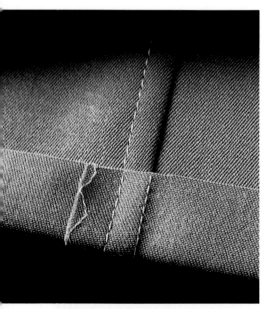

Welt seam has a tailored appearance and is often used for suits, coats, and pants. It's made like a mock flat-fell seam, except the final edgestitching is omitted. The single row of topstitching creates a slight ridge, making the seam pronounced and decorative.

Topstitched seam emphasizes attractive style lines in a garment. Use the width of the machine's presser foot as a guide to stitch ¼" (6 mm) on each side of a plain seam. Topstitch with contrasting thread or lustrous buttonhole twist to make seams focal points.

Overlocked seam is narrow, bound with overlocking stitches, and pressed to one side. Because the raw edges are trimmed as they are overlocked, be sure the garment fits before sewing. These seams are also called *merrow* or *serged* seams.

Collars

Collars are important details worthy of careful sewing. A well-made collar circles your neck without rippling or pulling and keeps its neat appearance through repeated cleanings. Pointed tips should match. Edges should be smooth and flat.

Interfacing, usually cut from the collar pattern piece, adds shape, support, and stability. Most collar styles benefit from the slightly firm finish provided by fusible interfacings. Select the special crisp type of fusible interfacing suitable for men's shirts if you are working with classic shirting fabrics such as oxford cloth or broadcloth. If your fabric is soft or delicate, like challis or crepe de chine, choose a lightweight fusible that bonds at low iron temperatures.

Convertible collar looks similar to the notched collar and lapels on a tailored blazer. The front facings fold back to form the lapels. This collar can be worn open or closed. The top button is usually omitted on casual wear.

Shirt collar with a stand comes from menswear traditions. There are two separate sections: the collar, and the *stand* between collar and neckline. In some patterns the stand is an extension of the collar section. This eliminates one seam and is faster to sew, but the sewing methods for both versions are similar. For a professional look, topstitch collar edges and stand seams close to the edge.

Standing collar may be shaped or cut double depth and folded along its length to form a self-facing.

Tips for Sewing Collars

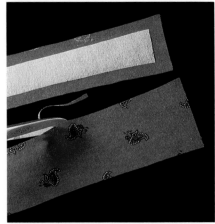

Trim outer edges of undercollar a scant ⅛" (3 mm) so the seam rolls toward the underside of the collar when stitched and turned. Pin right sides of collar and undercollar together with outer edges even.

Press collar seam open on a point presser; turn collar right side out. Gently push collar points out with a point turner. Press collar flat, allowing the seam to roll slightly toward the undercollar.

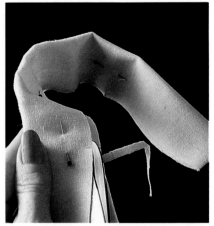

Roll collar into its finished position and pin. If necessary, trim raw edge of undercollar so it is even with upper collar edge. This makes the collar roll properly when it is sewn in place.

How to Attach a Convertible Collar

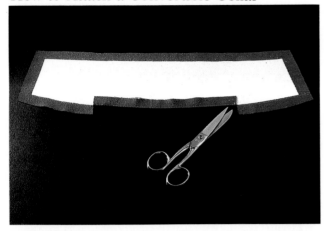

1) Staystitch upper collar neck seam before stitching to undercollar. Clip collar seam allowance to staystitching at shoulder marks. Press seam allowance to wrong side between clips.

2) Interface front facings up to foldline, using lined facing technique (page 108) or finishing facing edges with finish appropriate to fabric. Turn under facing seam allowances at shoulder seams; press.

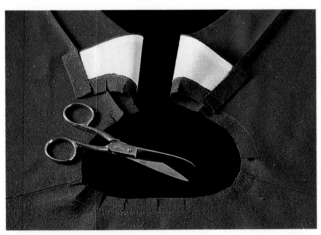

3) Stitch shoulder seams. Staystitch garment neck edge on seamline. Clip seam allowance at frequent intervals, stopping short of staystitching. Stitch upper and undercollars. Turn right side out, and press.

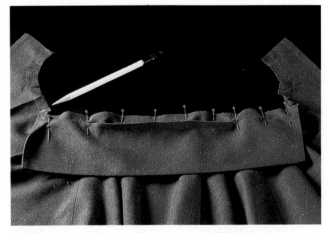

4) Pin undercollar only to garment between shoulder seams. Keep collar neck edge free. Pin upper collar and undercollar to front neck edge, matching markings.

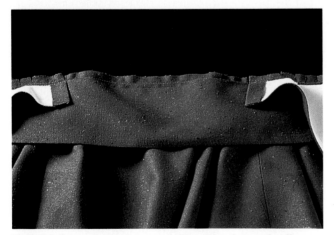

5) Fold front facings over collar. Pin through all layers. Stitch neckline seam, right side of garment up; do not catch folded edge of collar in stitching. Trim across corners, and grade seam; turn facings right side out.

6) Bring folded edge of upper collar over neck seam, and edgestitch or slipstitch in place. Slipstitch facings to shoulder seam allowances.

How to Attach a Shirt Collar with a Stand

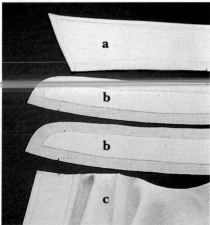

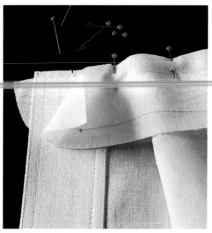

1) Topstitch outer edge of the collar (**a**). Interface both stand sections (**b**). Finish garment (**c**).

2) Pin the stand sections, right sides together, with shirt sandwiched between layers.

3) Stitch stand to neck seam. Stop ⅝" (1.5 cm) from stand edges (arrow). Trim and grade seam.

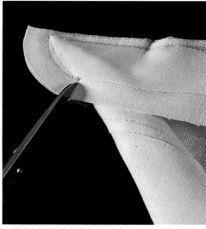

4) Roll shirt fronts out of the way of the curve at the front of the stand. Stitch curve from neck seam to collar placement mark.

5) Clip to seamline at marking. Trim curve; clip seams.

6) Turn stand right side out.

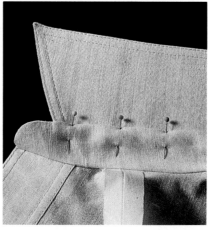

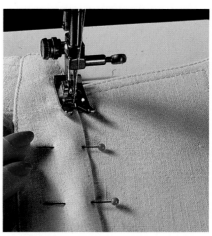

7) Stitch collar to right side of outside stand, with undercollar next to stand. Trim and grade seam; press seam toward stand.

8) Press under seam allowance of inside stand; trim to ¼" (6 mm). Pin pressed edge of stand to cover stitching line.

9) Edgestitch around stand through all fabric layers. Finished collar is shown on pages 32 and 33.

Standing Collar

A standing collar cut double forms a fold-over collar. The fold-over standing collar is often cut on the bias so the collar will stretch slightly to fit the contour of the neckline. When cutting on the bias, handle the fabric carefully to avoid twisting it. Cut knit standing collars on the crosswise ribs.

A standing collar cut as two pieces results in a straight or shaped band that stands at the neckline. Depending on the band, the collar may fit close to the neck like a shirt collar, or it may be a loose-fitting style.

Standing collars may be interfaced with a soft interfacing, such as a lightweight nonwoven interfacing that stretches slightly in all directions, a woven interfacing cut on the true bias grain, or fusible knit.

How to Attach a Standing Collar

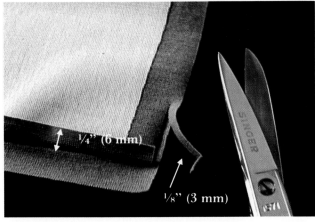

1) Interface collar and self-facing. Press self-facing neck seam allowance to wrong side, and trim to ¼" (6 mm). Fold collar in half lengthwise, and trim ⅛" (3 mm) from ends of self-facing.

2) Stitch short seams at collar ends. Trim and grade seams. Press seams open on point presser; turn collar right side out. After turning, press seams to roll toward facing.

3) Staystitch garment neck edge and clip curves as necessary. Stitch collar edge to garment. Trim and grade seam; press seam toward collar.

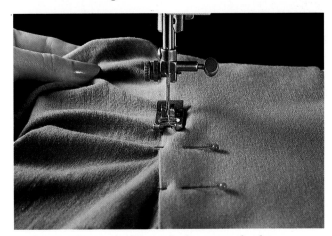

4) Turn collar to inside and pin pressed edge to cover seam. Edgestitch facing in place.

Yokes

A shirt or blouse yoke is a single section that fits straight across the back, just above the shoulder blades. Most yokes extend slightly below the shoulders in front. If so, the location of the shoulders is marked on the yoke pattern piece at neckline and armholes. Be sure to transfer these shoulder markings to the yoke after cutting. You'll need them to align collar and sleeves properly.

The direction of fabric grain on the yoke has a practical purpose. The strong lengthwise fabric grain runs along the back yoke seam, stabilizing the fabric where the shirt is subject to stress. Over the shoulders, the bias fabric grain naturally molds to figure contours.

Yokes are cut twice from the same pattern piece; one layer forms a lining for the other layer. When finished, a yoke has raw edges enclosed at the back and front seams. The sewing method given here comes from a classic technique for tailoring men's shirts. No machine stitching shows, inside or out.

How to Sew a Shirt Yoke

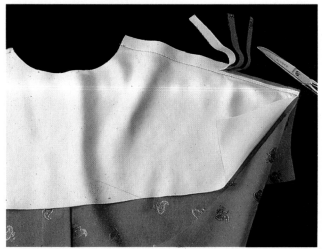

1) Stitch yoke and yoke lining to shirt fronts. Right sides of yoke and lining face each other; shirt fronts are sandwiched in between. Trim and grade seams.

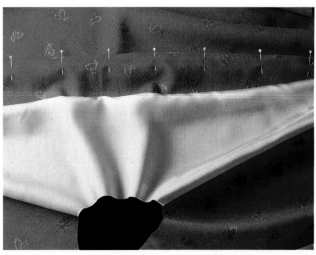

2) Pin back of shirt to yoke with right sides together. Yoke lining remains free.

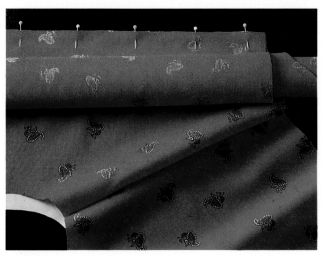

3) Roll the back of the shirt up to the pin-basted yoke seam. Roll shirt fronts up to shoulder seams.

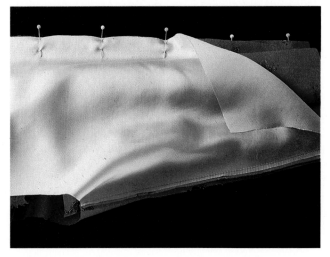

4) Bring yoke lining over rolled back and fronts. Match lining seam to pin-basted yoke seam; stitch. Trim and grade seam.

5) Reach through opening at neck to pull shirt sections out. Yoke will turn right side out.

6) Smooth out seams at shoulders and yoke; press.

Cuffs

Long sleeves on shirts, blouses, and lightweight jackets often have cuffs with buttoned closings. In many ways, sewing cuffs is similar to sewing collars. The tips on page 38 for trimming, interfacing, and pressing collars apply to cuffs, too.

Apply interfacing to half of a one-piece cuff. The interfaced half of the cuff shows on the outside of the finished sleeve. The half without interfacing is folded to the inside to form a self-facing. Interface one section of a two-piece cuff; this section belongs on the outside of the sleeve. The other cuff section forms the facing on the inside.

Apply cuffs, using either topstitching or hand finishing. Topstitching is usually faster, because it is done by machine. Cuffs without topstitching require hand finishing, but no stitches show on the outside.

Continuous bound placket is a slit bound with a strip of self-fabric. The binding strip is cut on the lengthwise fabric grain for stability. When the cuff is closed, this placket is hidden from view.

Shirt-style placket is a box-shaped sleeve opening finished with a shaped facing. The facing is folded and stitched so the edges of the placket overlap neatly. Adapted from menswear tailoring, this type of placket is found on patterns with traditional details. When the cuff is closed, the pointed portion of the facing shows on a shirt-style placket.

How to Sew a Continuous Bound Placket

1) Staystitch placket on seamline. Use short stitches on each side of placket point; take one stitch across point. Slash to stitch at point.

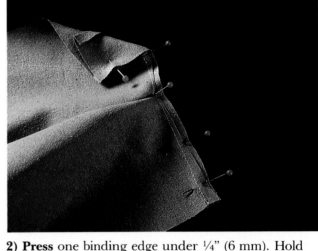

2) Press one binding edge under ¼" (6 mm). Hold slash straight to pin other binding edge to placket, right side of binding to wrong side of sleeve.

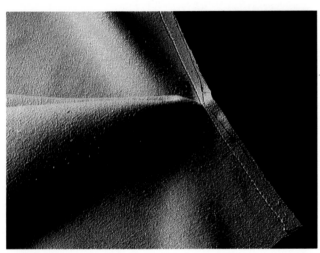

3) Stitch next to sleeve staystitching with ¼" (6 mm) seam allowance on placket; use presser foot as guide. Raw edges line up evenly only at seam ends.

4) Bring folded binding edge over seam. Fold should barely cover seam. Edgestitch fold through all layers of fabric; press.

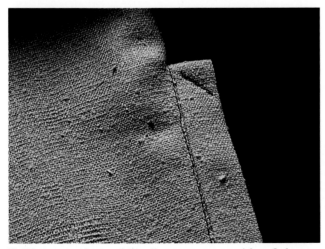

5) Line up edges of binding on wrong side of sleeve; stitch diagonally from top of binding to keep binding inside sleeve when cuff is finished.

6) Press binding flat on underlapping back placket edge. Press binding under on overlapping front placket edge. Attach cuff (page 47).

How to Sew a Shirt-style Placket

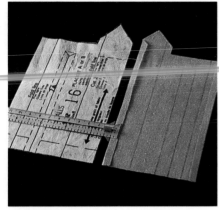

1) Press under ¼" (6 mm) seam allowances on sides of placket facing. Baste-mark across top of placket opening.

2) Press facing sides on foldlines. Facing edges should line up with marking for placket opening.

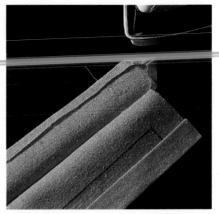

3) Press under seam allowances on point. Miter angled corners by folding seam allowance across point before folding side edges.

4) Match markings on facing and sleeve placket opening, right side of facing against wrong side of sleeve; stitch. Slash to ¼" (6 mm) from top, then clip to corners.

5) Pull facing through opening to right side of sleeve. Press seams toward placket opening. Press up triangle at top of placket.

6) Pin narrow facing edge to cover placket stitching; edgestitch inner fold of facing through all layers.

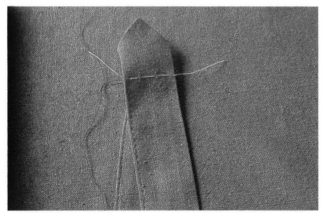

7) Fold other side of facing to cover placket stitching; pin. Edgestitch outer fold of overlap facing to top of opening. Pull threads to underside and tie.

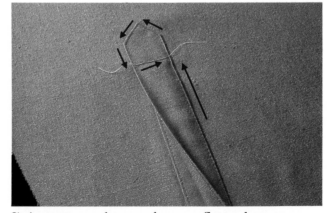

8) Arrange overlap so edges are flat and even. Edgestitch in direction of arrows, starting at lower edge, up around point, and across placket. Secure stitching. Finished placket is shown on pages 32 and 33.

How to Attach a Cuff

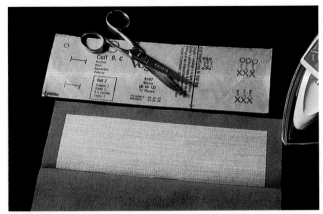

1) Fold cuff pattern in half and cut fusible interfacing from folded pattern, eliminating seam allowances. Fuse interfacing to upper cuff.

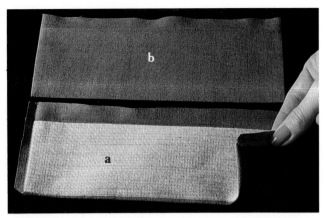

2) Press under seam allowance on interfaced edge. Fold cuff in half lengthwise, right sides together; stitch ends, opening out pressed seam allowance. Trim and grade seams. Press seams open **(a)**. Turn cuff right side out **(b)**.

3) Pin and stitch wrong side of sleeve to non-interfaced side of cuff, matching markings. Be sure ends of cuff are even with finished placket edges. Do not trim seam allowances.

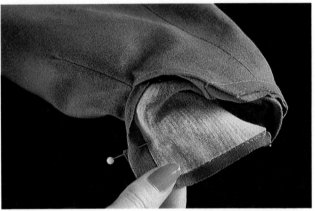

4) Wrap free cuff section around placket opening to front of sleeve as far as it will go. The right side of cuff is on right side of sleeve. Pin about 1" (2.5 cm) from placket opening.

5) Stitch pinned area at each end of cuff exactly on first stitching so first row will not show on outside. Trim seam close to stitching to eliminate bulk.

6) Turn cuff right side out; press. Right side of cuff edge is stitched to sleeve for about 1" (2.5 cm) next to placket opening.

7) Edgestitch folded edge of cuff over seam. Topstitch ¼" (6 mm) from edge of cuff. For a cuff that is not topstitched, attach to right side of sleeve, turn to inside, and slipstitch in place.

Sleeves

Whether short or long, all sleeves are one of three basic styles: set-in, kimono, or raglan.

Set-in sleeves have a rounded cap that is larger than the corresponding part of the armhole. The cap must be eased to fit smoothly into place. As a softer fashion detail, set-in sleeves may also have gathers or pleats in the sleeve cap. The traditional method of setting in sleeves uses two rows of easestitching on the sleeve to fit the cap into place. If you've had some sewing experience, you may prefer an alternate way (page 50) that eliminates easestitching. The flat method, opposite, is used for a man-tailored shirt sleeve, which has less ease than classic set-in styles. The sleeve is inserted before the sleeve or garment side seams are stitched.

Kimono sleeves extend without seams from garment front and back sections. Shoulder shaping is rounded, as in raglan sleeves. Kimono sleeves are often loosely fitted and drape softly under the arms. Even loose-fitting kimono sleeves are subject to stress in the underarm area. Reinforce this curved seam with tape, two rows of stitching, shortened stitches, or a reinforcing stretch stitch.

Raglan sleeves have a slanted seam in the front and the back. Most raglan sleeves have a seam that curves over the shoulder and extends the length of the sleeve. This seam shapes the shoulder in a rounded way. In some patterns darts, instead of seams, shape the shoulders. For more comfort and better fit, stitch the sleeve and side seam before setting in the sleeve.

Shaping aids, such as sleeve puffs and shoulder pads, are needed to complete some sleeve treatments. Sleeve puffs are small pads that support gathered sleeve caps. Puffs lift gathers so the sleeve hangs straight and smooth. An easy method for making puffs is given on page 51.

Tips for Sewing Sleeves

Pattern markings such as notches, dots, and shoulder seam marks help to position set-in sleeve. More fabric must be eased at the back of the sleeve than at the front. No fabric should be eased into the armhole at the top of the sleeve cap for 1" (2.5 cm) at center dot.

Notches on pattern pieces tell which way sleeve and armhole edges should face. Double notches indicate the back of the sleeve and armhole. A single notch indicates the front. Mark notches with ¼" (6 mm) snips into the seam allowance.

How to Sew a Shirt Sleeve (flat method)

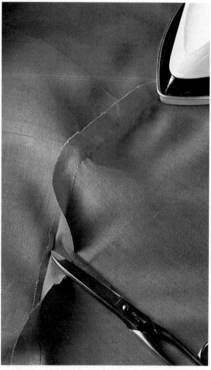

1) Pin sleeve to armhole, right sides together, matching notches and small dots. Pin on garment side, easing sleeve cap to fit.

2) Stitch sleeve to armhole with garment side up. Action of feed eases sleeve to fit armhole.

3) Press seam away from sleeve. Trim garment seam allowance to ¼" (6 mm) for mock flat-fell seam.

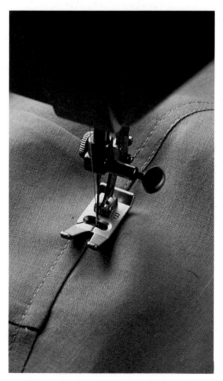

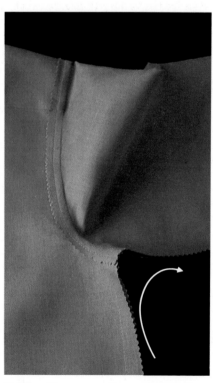

4) Topstitch sleeve seam on the right side of garment ¼" (6 mm) from the seamline.

5) Edgestitch close to seamline.

6) Pin side seam of garment and sleeve together. Stitch in one continuous seam. Reinforce underarm area with short stitches, or use mock flat-fell seam.

How to Sew a Set-in Sleeve without Easestitching

1) Pin sleeve to armhole at underarm seam, small dots, double notches, top of sleeve, and single notches. Pin from garment side.

2) Stitch underarm seam from notch to notch, garment side up. Hold edges together with your fingers as you stitch the sleeve in place.

3) Ease sleeve to armhole, starting at a notch. With thumb, press fabric firmly behind presser foot, forcing fabric to pile up. Release and repeat every 1" to 2" (2.5 to 5 cm). Action of feed eases sleeve evenly.

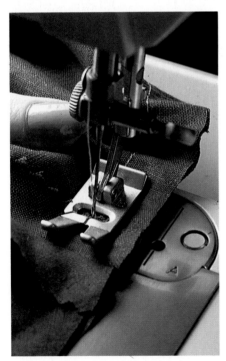

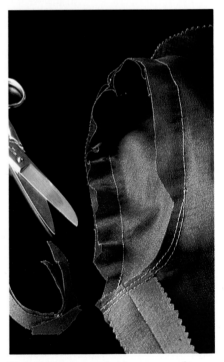

4) Release thumb ½" (1.3 cm) from marking at top of sleeve, allowing fabric to feed normally. No fabric should be eased for 1" (2.5 cm) at top of sleeve.

5) Repeat easestitching on other side of sleeve to single or double notch, as in step 3, above. Less fabric is eased in sleeve front than in sleeve back.

6) Reinforce underarm seam by stitching a second row between notches. Trim underarm area between notches.

How to Sew a Gathered Sleeve with a Sleeve Puff

1) Machine-baste between gathering marks on sleeve cap. Stitch one row on seamline; stitch second row ¼" (6 mm) from first, in seam allowance. Stitch sleeve seam; press open.

2) Pull up both bobbin threads on each side of sleeve cap to make gathers. Pin sleeve into armhole, matching markings. Distribute gathers evenly, and pin in place on sleeve side.

3) Stitch on seamline, adjusting gathers evenly. Remove pins as you come to them. In seam allowance, stitch again ¼" (6 mm) from seamline. Trim underarm seam between notches.

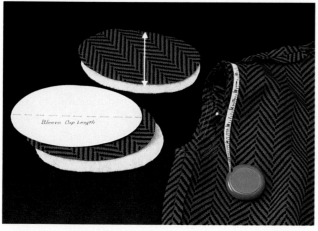

4) Cut oval puff from fashion fabric, long enough to fit top of sleeve and about 4½" (11.5 cm) wide. True bias grain (arrow) runs across oval. Cut an oval filler from fleece or quilt batting.

5) Fold curved edges of puff over filler, wrong sides together. Stitch ¼" (6 mm) seam through all layers.

6) Trim filler from seam allowance.

7) Stitch puff to seam allowance of sleeve cap.

8) Puff lifts gathers and supports sleeve at sleeve cap.

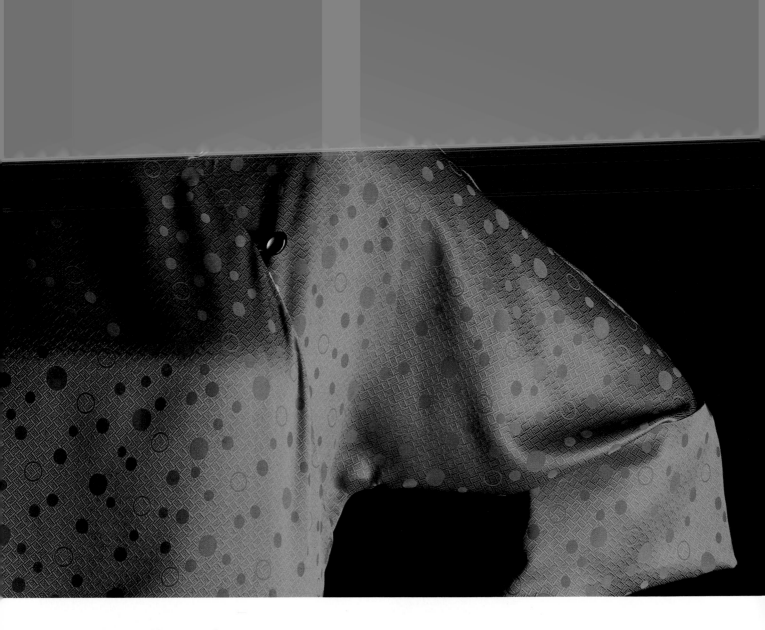

How to Sew a Kimono Sleeve

1) Pin narrow tape over seamline at underarm. Twill, bias, or seam tape can be used.

2) Stitch underarm seam, catching tape in stitches. Reinforce curve with short stitches. Clip curve, but do not clip into tape. Press seam open over tailor's ham.

Alternative method: Omit step 1. Stitch, clip, and press seam as in step 2. Center tape over curved area of seam. Stitch on both sides and across ends of tape, stitching through all layers of fabric.

How to Sew a Raglan Sleeve

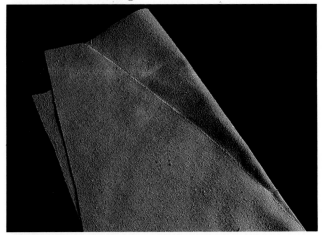

1) Stitch shoulder dart in sleeve. (Some raglan sleeves have a shoulder seam here instead of a dart.)

2) Trim dart to ½" (1.3 cm) and press open over a tailor's ham.

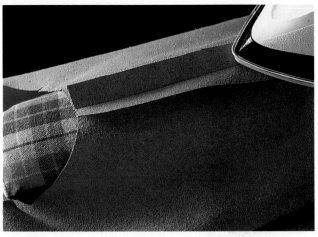

3) Stitch sleeve underarm seam. Press seam open.

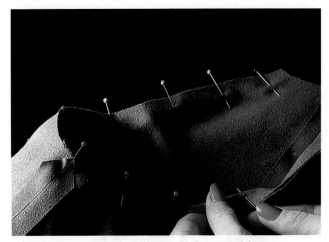

4) Pin sleeve to garment armhole, matching underarm seams and pattern markings. Trim cross seams diagonally at underarm.

5) Stitch armhole seam with sleeve side up. Begin at one neckline edge and stitch to other neckline edge.

6) Reinforce underarm area between notches with second row of stitches ¼" (6 mm) from seam. Trim underarm seam close to stitches; press toward sleeve. Press seam open above notches.

Shoulder Pads

Shoulder pads are a necessity when listed on the pattern envelope as a notion because the designer has included the pads as a fashion styling detail. If you omit them, the sleeves and shoulder seams will droop and wrinkle.

Shoulder pads should match pattern silhouette, the outline of the fashion. Purchased pads are available in two general types, triangular and raglan, but there are many variations within these two groups. The thickness may vary from ¼" (6 mm) for slight padding to 1" (2.5 cm) for more exaggerated shaping. They are usually made of a nonwoven fleece or fiberfill. Do not be afraid to trim the size or shape, or remove some of the filling. This customizes a purchased pad to fit your figure and the garment.

Triangular pads sit on top of the shoulders. Use these pads to shape a crisp, squared-off shoulder line. The most common use for triangular pads is for classic set-in sleeves. Patterns with extended shoulder seams should also have these pads.

Raglan pads cup over the shoulders. Use these pads for raglan, kimono, and set-in sleeves with dropped shoulders, as well as any other shoulder outline that is rounded.

Whenever shoulder pads are used in unlined garments, they can be covered with a self-fabric (if lightweight) or lining fabric, for a couture look. Lightweight pads covered with a lining fabric may also be purchased for use in unlined blouses or dresses. To make a custom shoulder pad for a lined garment, follow the instructions on page 89.

In the photos below, the left side has the pad in the proper position. The right side shows the appropriate pad and its proper placement.

Shoulder Pad Placement

Set-in sleeve. Try on the garment, and place the triangular shoulder pad in position. Extend the pad about ⅜" (1 cm) from the seamline, into the sleeve. Pin in place along the shoulder seam.

Kimono or raglan sleeve. Place raglan pad so it extends over the shoulder, creating a soft, rounded look. Tack to shoulder seam only, or attach with hook and loop tape to make pad removable.

Gathered set-in sleeve. Use triangular pad, extended 1" (2.5 cm) into the sleeve cap to shape and support the gathers. Sleeve puff may also be used to lift and hold gathers.

Extended or dropped shoulder. Raglan pad should cup over the shoulder. If using triangular pad, extend it at least 1" (2.5 cm) beyond normal shoulder line into sleeve cap to round the silhouette.

How to Cover a Shoulder Pad with Fashion Fabric

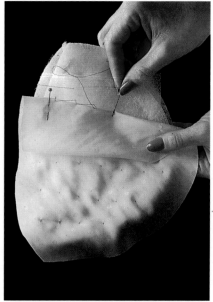

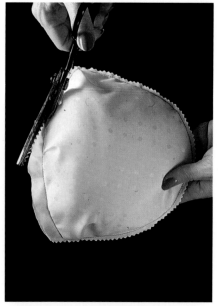

1) Make pattern by tracing around shoulder pad. Cut two pieces (for two pads) for inner lining, adding ½" (1.3 cm) seam allowance. Cut two pieces for outer lining, adding 1" (2.5 cm) seam allowance.

2) Place smaller lining piece on inner curve of pad. Starting on left side, fold lining back and attach with slanted basting stitches between pad and lining so short stitches are on lining side. Fold lining down over pad so next row of stitching is 1½" (3.8 cm) from first. Continue across pad.

3) Pin larger lining piece to upper curve of pad, easing in fullness and taking small tucks if necessary. Do not pull too tight. Stitch around pad by hand or machine. Trim edges evenly, and pink or zigzag edges together.

Three Ways to Attach Shoulder Pads

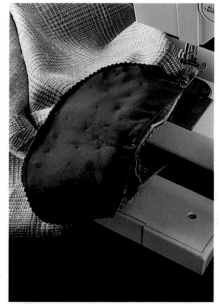

Hand-tack triangular shoulder pad in set-in sleeve at three points on armhole seam: top of sleeve cap, armhole back, and armhole front. Then tack tip of pad to shoulder seam allowances. Allow some slack in hand stitches. Do not sew pads rigidly into place.

Machine-tack triangular shoulder pad at same points described for hand tacking, left. Use a wide, closely spaced zigzag stitch. To work by machine, tack shoulder tip first, stitching through pad and seam allowances only.

Hook and loop tape makes shoulder pad removable to clean or press garment. Use lightweight tape. For either triangular or raglan pad, stitch loop half of tape to shoulder seam allowances, and hook half to shoulder pad. No tacking is needed at armhole.

Pockets

Pockets vary in purpose from practical to decorative. Practical pockets usually are simple in style. Yet the shape, decorative trim, or position of a pocket can make it a fashion focus. To be useful, however, pockets should fall comfortably within hand's reach, even if this means adjusting the pattern.

Choose a sturdy, firmly woven fabric for hidden pocket sections of in-seam and slanted pocket styles. The pocket is less likely to wear out if cut from fabric such as cotton twill or drill cloth. Tailors use *pocketing*, a special lightweight twill, for pockets on pants and jackets. A durable lining fabric is also a good choice.

Patch pockets are sewn to the outside of a garment. Pocket edges should be neat, smooth, and securely applied. They may be interfaced for stability, lined, or self-lined on tailored lined garments.

In-seam pockets are hidden pockets. From the outside of a garment they look like an opening in a seam.

Slanted pockets open diagonally from the waist to the sides of pants and skirts.

Welt pockets are hidden pockets with a visible slit. They may have a single or double welt and are sometimes covered with a flap.

Patch Pockets

As outside details, patch pockets add fashion detail to a garment. Position them where they look best on your figure. Try pockets above, below, or beside the placement line on the pattern to find the most flattering position that will avoid calling attention to full bust or hips.

Once you've determined the position for pockets, double-check the placement before attaching them. Measure carefully so pockets are precisely aligned. This step is especially important when pockets are symmetrical because a minor pattern adjustment can affect pocket alignment.

Patch pockets may be applied by hand or machine stitching. Choose the machine method for casual garments, as a time-saving technique, and for the most secure application. If you prefer a fine, invisible finish, sew the pockets in place by hand.

Interface patch pockets with a lightweight fusible interfacing for smooth shape and longer wear. Cut the interfacing to the hem fold at the pocket top and to the seamline at the sides and bottom of the pocket. Avoid a too-stiff pocket by cutting woven interfacings on the true bias grain.

Reinforce patch pockets at the upper corners. Stitch small triangles on man-tailored shirts and sportswear. Use fine zigzag stitches for bar tacks on children's clothes and rugged outdoor wear. Topstitching may be added for further reinforcement.

How to Sew a Patch Pocket with Square Corners

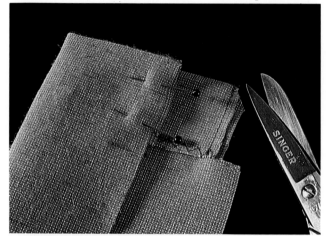

1) Finish upper edge of pocket. Fold hem to outside. Pull hem edges ⅛" (3 mm) beyond pocket so seams will roll toward inside. Stitch on seamline. Trim corners diagonally; grade seams.

2) Turn hem right side out, using point turner to push out corners. Press seam allowances under on sides and lower edges.

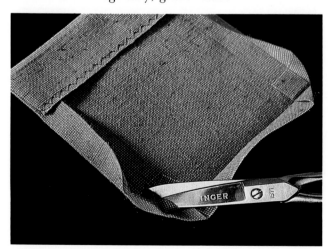

3) Fold seam allowance diagonally across lower corners so pressed foldlines match. Press diagonal folds, then trim to ¼" (6 mm).

4) Press seam allowance again to inside, forming miter at corners. Trim remaining seam allowances. Edgestitch or topstitch if desired.

How to Sew a Patch Pocket with Rounded Corners

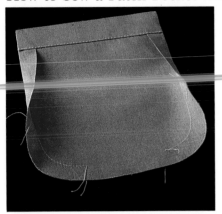

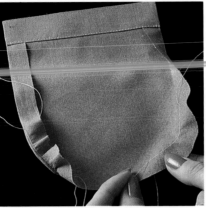

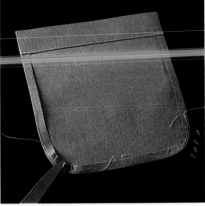

1) Stitch upper hem as for patch pocket, page 57, step 1. Also easestitch around corners, just inside seamline.

2) Press seam allowance to inside of pocket. Pull thread at corner stitches to ease in extra seam allowance evenly.

3) Trim entire seam allowance to ¼" (6 mm). If necessary, notch out fullness at corner curves to make seam allowance lie flat.

How to Sew a Lined Patch Pocket

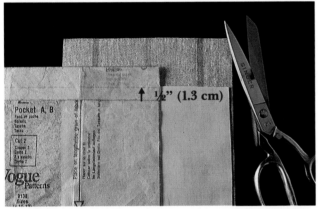

↑ ½" (1.3 cm)

1) Fold hem down on pocket pattern. Mark lining cutting line ½" (1.3 cm) from upper edge of pattern. Cut lining ⅛" (3 mm) smaller on sides and bottom.

2) Stitch top of lining to top of pocket, right sides together, with ¼" (6 mm) seam. Leave opening for turning at center of seam (arrows). Press seam open.

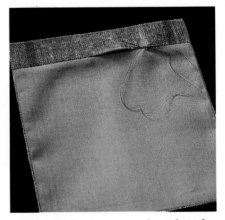

3) Bring lower edge of lining and pocket together. Stitch side and lower edges. Trim seams and corners; notch fullness from curves of rounded pockets.

4) Turn pocket right side out through opening in seam. Press pocket from lining side, rolling seam toward back of pocket.

5) Slipstitch seam opening closed.

How to Sew a Self-lined Patch Pocket

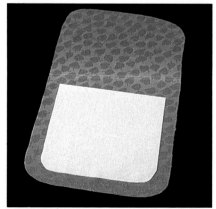

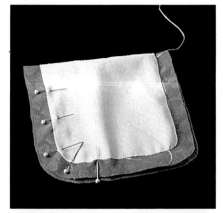

1) Fold pocket pattern on hemline. Place pattern fold on fabric fold, and cut double pocket. Fuse interfacing on one half of pocket.

2) Pin right sides together, pulling non-interfaced side ⅛" (3 mm) beyond edge. Stitch seam; trim and notch. Cut 1" (2.5 cm) bias slit on non-interfaced side of pocket.

3) Turn pocket to right side through slit. Press edges, rolling seam to side with slit in it. Close slit with fusible interfacing inserted adhesive side up.

How to Apply a Patch Pocket by Machine

1) Transfer pocket placement line to right side of garment with machine basting.

2) Use basting tape, pins, or glue, to hold pocket in place over the baste-marked line.

3) Edgestitch pocket to garment. Reinforce upper corners with stitched triangles or bar tacks.

How to Apply a Patch Pocket by Hand

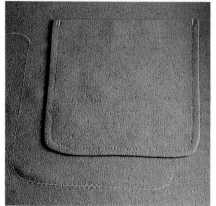

1) Topstitch pocket before applying pocket to garment. Baste-mark pocket placement line as in machine method above, step 1.

2) Hand-baste pocket in position, stitching along pocket edge to use as guideline on wrong side.

3) Backstitch pocket in place, working from inside of garment. Stitching should not show from right side.

In-Seam Pockets

There are three ways of cutting in-seam pockets: cutting the pocket as a part of a garment, cutting a separate pocket, and cutting a garment extension plus a separate pocket. Sewing an in-seam pocket that is a part of the garment eliminates one seam but can create unwanted bulk unless the garment fabric is lightweight. Cutting a separate pocket reduces bulk because you can use a lining fabric.

How to Sew an In-Seam Pocket

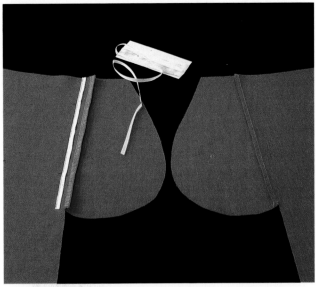

1) Edgestitch tape on wrong side in seam allowance of front pocket extension. Stitch pockets to front and back extensions. Trim seam to ¼" (6 mm). Zigzag edges together; press toward pocket.

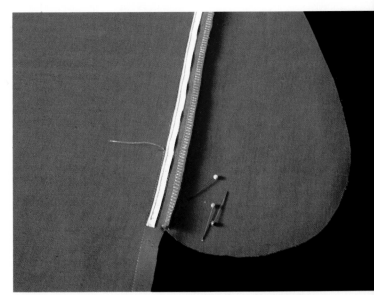

2) Pin garment front to garment back; machine-baste pocket opening closed. Stitch pocket and garment seam above and below pocket opening. Use short reinforcement stitches, and backstitch at opening.

How to Sew an In-Seam Pocket in a Mock Flat-fell Seam

1) Follow steps 1 and 2, above, for in-seam pocket. On garment back only, clip seam at top and bottom of pocket (arrow). Trim side seam allowance on garment front to ¼" (6 mm) for mock flat-fell seam.

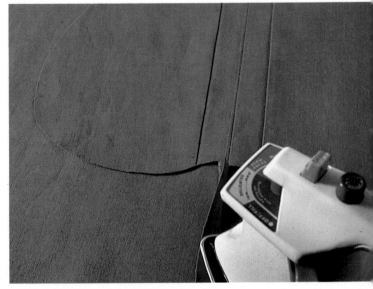

2) Press seam toward front, above and below clips on back pocket. Press pocket sections open so front pocket folds over garment front, and back pocket folds over garment back.

The third method, using an extension, reduces bulk and prevents the pocket lining from showing on the curve of the hip. To prevent pocket opening from stretching when pockets are cut separately, stitch narrow twill or seam tape in the seam allowance of the front pocket.

Topstitching helps to hold the pocket in place and flattens any bulk at the seam, giving a slimmer line in the hip area. It is used below for an in-seam pocket with a mock flat-fell seam.

3) Stitch around pocket, ending at side seam. Clip seam above and below extension on back garment section only, so seam can be pressed open.

4) Press garment seam open above and below clips. Press pocket toward garment front. Finish raw edges of pocket together. Remove basting stitches.

3) Topstitch entire garment seam ¼" (6 mm) from seamline. Edgestitch next to seam.

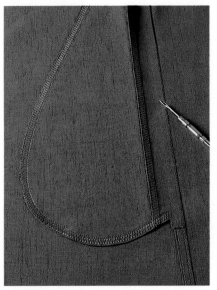

4) Fold the back pocket over the front pocket, and pin together. Stitch. Finish raw edges, and remove basting stitches.

5) Edgestitching and topstitching on right side of garment continue across pocket edge.

Slanted Pockets

Slanted pockets are formed from two pattern pieces: the pocket and the garment side front. The side front fills in the hip area of the garment above the pocket opening and completes the inside of the pocket. The pocket pattern can be cut from lining fabric to minimize bulk because the pocket is hidden on the inside.

How to Sew a Slanted Pocket

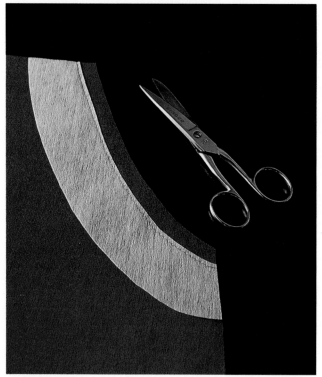

1) Cut 2" (5 cm) strip of sew-in interfacing to match shape of curved pocket edges. Stitch ½" (1.3 cm) from edge on wrong side. Trim interfacing. If edge is straight, instead of interfacing stitch seam tape over pocket seamline to stabilize bias grainline.

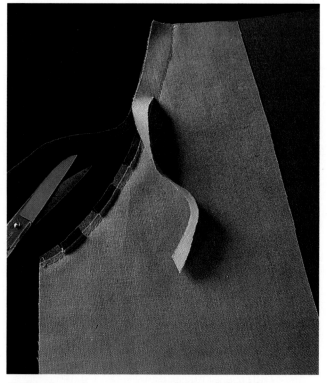

2) Stitch pocket to garment front, right sides together. Trim seam, grading so pocket seam allowance is narrower. Clip curves.

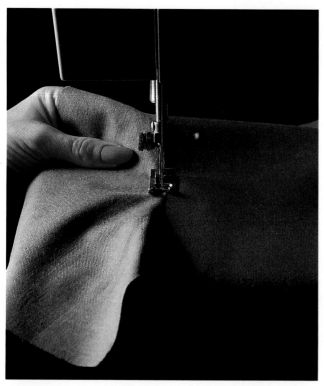

3) Press seam toward pocket. If pocket will not be topstitched, understitch seam on pocket side to prevent pocket from rolling to right side.

4) Fold pocket to inside. Press pocket edge, rolling seam toward pocket. Topstitch or edgestitch edge of pocket if it has not been understitched.

5) Stitch side front of garment to pocket. Finish raw edges with zigzag stitches or another edge finish (pages 36 and 37).

6) Baste pocket to garment at side seam and at waist seam. Use pattern markings to line up fabric layers. Pocket should lie flat without ripples.

Welt Pockets

Double welt pockets look like large bound buttonholes. A *welt,* which is a narrow, folded strip of garment fabric, finishes each edge of the pocket opening. The pocket, cut from a lining fabric, extends from the welts on the inside of the garment. Double welt pockets can also be made with a flap (page 69).

Making welt pockets is an expert tailoring technique that requires precise marking, cutting, and stitching. Before starting, carefully check the pocket position. Once you have started making the pocket, recheck the pocket position before slashing the welt. In the photos, the wrong side of the garment has been backed with fusible interfacing.

How to Cut and Prepare a Pocket Lining

1) Cut the following pocket parts 7" by 3" (18 by 7.5 cm) for finished 5" (12.5 cm) welt: **(a)** pocket stay, from nonwoven sew-in interfacing; **(b)** welt and **(c)** pocket facing, from fashion fabric; **(d)** interfacing, from weft insertion fusible. Cut lining **(e)** 7" by 12" to 15" (18 by 30.5 to 38 cm).

2) Fuse interfacing to wrong side of welt. Place welt **(f)**, right side up, on one edge of pocket lining. Zigzag inner edge of welt to lining. Machine-baste outer edge of welt to lining. Stitch pocket facing **(g)** to other edge of lining as for welt. Upper interfaced part of lining will be welt. Lower non-interfaced part will be inside of pocket.

How to Sew a Welt Pocket

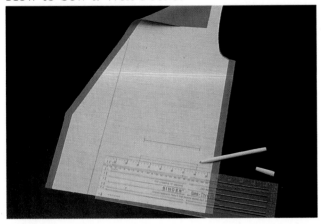

1) Mark pocket placement line on wrong side of garment. Mark center of stay. Draw pocket stitching box with lines ¼" (6 mm) from center line. Mark ends with short vertical lines 5" (12.5 cm) apart, 1" (2.5 cm) from ends of stay.

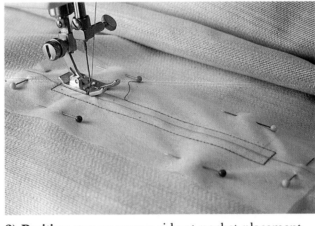

2) Position stay on wrong side at pocket placement marking. Sew around entire box, using small stitches and beginning on one long side. This transfers pocket stitching box to right side. Do not backstitch.

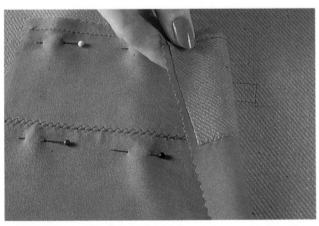

3) Pin right side of welt/pocket section to right side of garment, centering welt over baste-marked pocket stitching box.

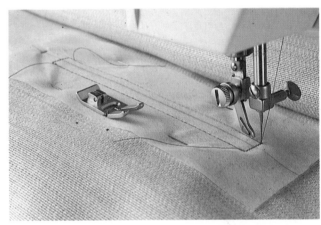

4) Stitch long sides only of pocket stitching box, working from wrong side of garment. Stop exactly at end marks on box, backstitching to secure threads. (Presser foot has been removed to show where stitching ends.)

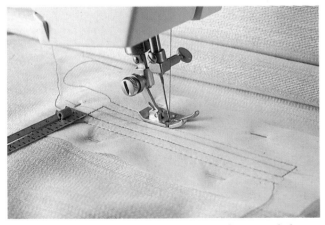

5) Machine-baste exactly ¼" (6 mm) from each long side of pocket stitching box, working from wrong side of garment. Use width of presser foot as stitching guide.

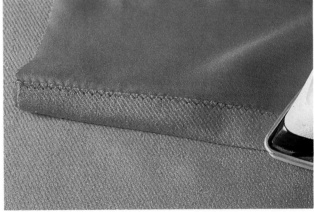

6) Press welt/pocket section up, working from right side of garment. Press firmly to create neat, flat fold. Pin. Lower line of machine basting is inside this fold.

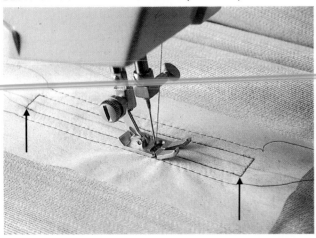

7) Stitch on lower long line of pocket stitching box from wrong side of garment. Stop exactly at end marks (arrow); backstitch to secure threads. This forms lower welt.

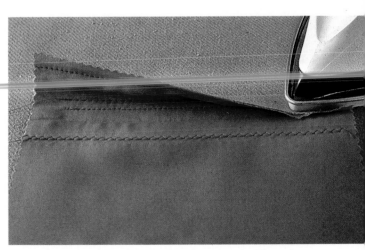

8) Press welt/pocket section down. Upper line of machine basting is inside fold.

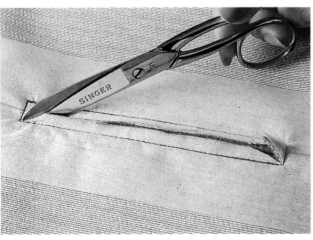

11) Cut through center of pocket stitching box from wrong side of garment. Stop ⅝" (1.5 cm) from each end, then cut diagonally to each corner, forming triangles. Be careful to cut *garment* fabric only.

12) Turn welts and pocket to wrong side by pulling them through pocket opening. Make sure triangles are pulled through and folded flat between welts and pocket stay. Press.

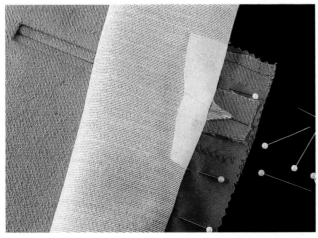

15) Fold garment back out of the way to prepare for stitching pocket side seams.

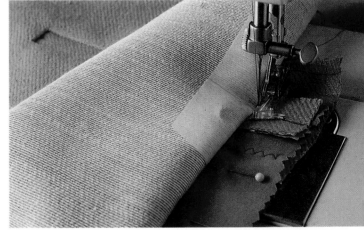

16) Stitch pocket side seams, using zipper foot; stitch close to fold of triangles at ends of pocket opening.

9) Stitch on upper long line of pocket stitching box from wrong side of garment; backstitch to secure threads. This forms upper welt.

10) Slash welt by cutting through center of welt between stitching rows. *Do not* cut into garment. Remove bastestitching from upper and lower welt.

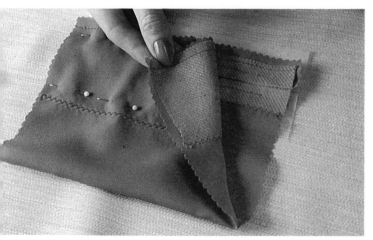

13) Fold pocket up so pocket facing covers welts. Pin facing to top of welt.

14) Stitch in the ditch of upper welt from right side of garment, using zipper foot. Stitch through all layers. This also secures pocket lining to welt.

17) Press pocket lining so it lies flat.

18) Whipstitch edges of upper and lower welts together to hold pocket opening in place while you sew the remainder of garment.

Pocket Flaps

Welt and patch pockets can be covered with flaps. Make the flap after sewing the pocket to be sure that a patch pocket flap is at least ¼" (6 mm) larger than the pocket or that the welt pocket flap is at least ⅛" (3 mm) shorter than the pocket opening.

Flaps may be faced with a lining fabric to eliminate bulk. Trim ⅛" (3 mm) from the sides and lower edge of the facing; when the flap is turned to the right side, the seam will roll under the flap.

Select a fusible interfacing that will result in a crisp, well-defined edge. Trim seam allowances from interfacing before fusing.

How to Sew a Pocket Flap

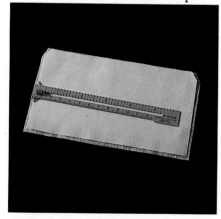

1) Fuse crisp interfacing to wrong side of flap. Trim ⅛" (3 mm) from sides and lower edge of flap lining. Pin facing and flap together, outer edges even. Pocket flap is larger than lining.

2) Stitch on seamline, shortening stitches on curve or taking short diagonal stitch across square corners. Trim and grade seams; clip curves as necessary.

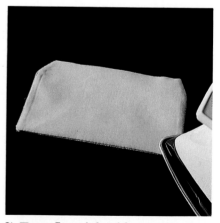

3) Turn flap right side out. Press flap from wrong side, rolling seam toward lining. Topstitch or edgestitch if desired.

How to Attach a Flap to a Patch Pocket

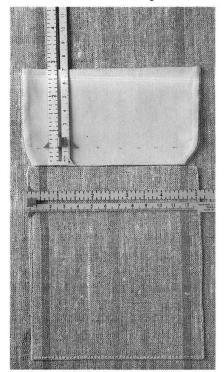  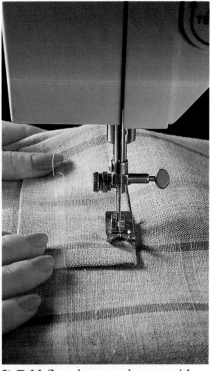

1) Position flap above pocket with flap seamline ½" (1.3 cm) above the pocket. Be sure flap extends ⅛" (3 mm) on each side of pocket.

2) Stitch flap in place; backstitch at each end. Trim seam to scant ¼" (6 mm).

3) Fold flap down and press with press cloth. Topstitch ¼" (6 mm) from fold. Do not backstitch. Pull thread ends to inside and tie.

How to Attach a Flap to a Welt Pocket

 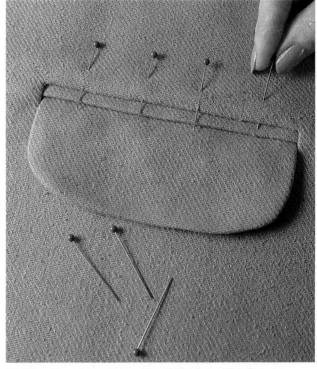

1) Complete welt pocket through step 13, pages 65 to 67. Measure pocket opening to determine length of flap; flap should be ⅛" (3 mm) shorter than opening. Make flap, steps 1 to 3, opposite.

2) Slip flap through pocket opening. Pin flap in position between top welt and folded-up pocket, aligning flap seam with upper welt seam. Complete welt pocket, pages 66 and 67, steps 14 to 18.

Waistbands & Waistlines

A waistband is a separate strip of fabric that finishes pants and skirts at the waistline. A well-made waistband needs interfacing or other inside support to keep it from stretching and wrinkling. The technique shown here uses *non-roll woven waistbanding*, a crisp, woven stiffener that creates a firm, smooth waistband. Purchase waistbanding stiffener to match the finished width of the garment waistband. The stiffener is prefinished on its long edges, which should not be cut or trimmed.

A waistline is a horizontal seam that joins the bodice of a garment to the lower section. This seam usually falls at your natural waist; however, depending on the fashion design, the seam could also fall above or below your natural waist.

Expert sewing at the waistline means carefully trimming and grading the layers of fabric to eliminate a bulky appearance, pressing the area, and stabilizing it to prevent stretching.

A simple technique is to use elastic at the waistline. With this method the waist area is adjustable and comfortable, and good fit is easy to achieve. A method for closely fitted waistlines in fabrics that may stretch is to use a *waistline stay,* a strong tape or ribbon reinforcement to prevent the waistline from stretching out of shape. Use ½" (1.3 cm) wide twill tape, woven seam tape, or grosgrain ribbon.

How to Sew a Waistband with Non-roll Woven Waistbanding

1) Cut woven waistband stiffener the length of garment waistband, minus seam allowances at waistband ends. Cut waistband with 3/8" (1 cm) seam allowance on one long edge.

2) Finish one long edge of waistband with zigzag. Stitch waistband to garment, right sides together.

3) Lap stiffener over waistline seam allowances; edgestitch, lining up edge of stiffener with waist seamline. At ends of waistband, stiffener stops at seamlines, not at raw edges.

4) Grade waistband seam. Trim garment seam allowance close to edgestitching. Trim waistband seam allowance to 1/4" (6 mm). Press waistband up.

5) Fold waistband along its length, right sides together. Top of waistband should extend slightly beyond stiffener. Stitch across ends. Trim seams.

6) Turn band right side out. Press waistband over stiffener. Pin, baste, or glue in place. From right side, stitch in the ditch, catching finished edge.

How to Sew an Elasticized Waistline

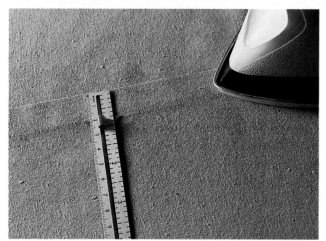

1) Machine-stitch upper and lower sections of garment together, using a ¾" (2 cm) seam allowance. Press seam allowances up.

2) Trim seam allowance of bodice to ¼" (6 mm) to reduce bulk. Press remaining seam allowance under ¼" (6 mm).

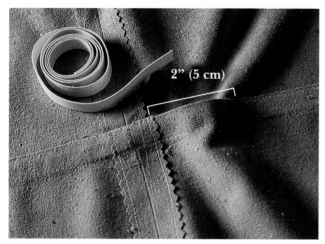

2" (5 cm)

3) Edgestitch folded seam allowance to bodice, leaving a 2" (5 cm) opening.

4) Insert elastic into casing; join ends. Machine-stitch opening while pulling elastic taut.

How to Stitch and Stay a Waistline Seam

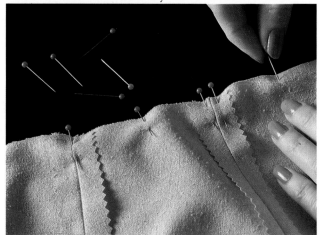

1) Pin bodice inside skirt, right sides together; match seamlines, notches, and markings. Ease skirt to fit as you pin.

2) Stitch waistline seam with bodice side up.

3) Trim ends of darts, pleats, and seams diagonally. Grade trimmed layers of darts and pleats so layer next to garment is slightly wider.

4) Baste stay or seam tape to garment waistline with one edge of stay on waist seamline. With skirt side up, stitch stay to waist seam allowance just above waistline seam.

5) Grade seam allowances. Trim bodice seam allowance to width of stay; trim skirt seam allowance ¼" (6 mm) narrower. If fabric ravels, zigzag stay and raw edges of seam together.

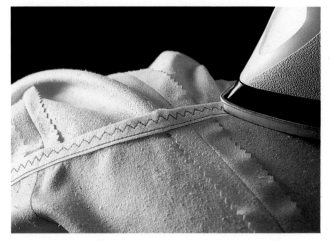

6) Press seam flat to blend stitches and smooth out eased areas. Press seam up toward bodice. Avoid flattening gathers or pleats below seamline.

Tailoring with Fusible Interfacings

Tailoring differs from dressmaking in a number of ways. The term *tailored* applies to fashions styled like menswear, such as a suit jacket. It also describes certain methods of construction and pattern design. The undercollar and collar on a tailored jacket, for example, are cut from two different pattern pieces to shape the collar. In dressmaking, both collar layers are usually cut from the same pattern piece. Details such as a welt pocket, notched collar, and full lining are typical in patterns for tailored fashions.

Tailoring also calls for extensive use of interfacings for building in shape. Entire garment sections, not just the details, are backed with interfacing when tailored. Two layers of interfacing may be used for shaping the roll line on jacket lapels. Because different kinds of interfacings have distinctive effects, a single tailored jacket may require several types of interfacing.

Fusible interfacings have eliminated most of the time-consuming handwork that was once the trademark of tailoring. With fusibles you can tailor

expertly with just a little practice. However, it's important to choose the right fashion fabric and interfacing for the tailoring task at hand.

Using Fusible Interfacings

Four types of fusible interfacings may be used for tailoring; often all four are used in one garment. *Fusible tricot,* a knitted interfacing, adds body and support to the fabric without causing stiffness. Use it to stabilize garment sections such as sleeves, hems, front facings, and the upper collar. *Fusible hair canvas,* a woven interfacing, is firm and resilient. Use it for the jacket front and undercollar when the fabric needs strong support. *Weft insertion fusible* is a knitted interfacing with extra yarns inserted crosswise. In a medium weight, it is a softer alternative to hair canvas and is used to stabilize fashion details, such as vents on jacket hems and the roll lines of lapels and undercollars. In a lighter weight, it is an alternative to fusible tricot. *Crisp,*

nonwoven fusible interfacing is used to keep small details, such as pocket flaps, firm and smooth.

Test fusible interfacings by making a sample when tailoring. Because entire sections of the garment will be interfaced, the sample should be large enough to drape over your hand, at least 6" (15 cm) square (larger if you can spare the fabric). The ideal method for testing fusible interfacings is to fuse 6" (15 cm) squares of different types of interfacing on a long panel, leaving plain fabric in between. The contrast in feeling between interfaced and non-interfaced areas clearly shows the effect of each interfacing.

Choosing Tailoring Fabrics

When tailoring with fusible interfacings, you'll be more satisfied if you begin with a durable fabric of good quality. Natural fiber fabrics, such as wool, cotton, silk, and linen, respond well to fusing. Many fabrics made from synthetic fibers and blends, such as polyester and rayon, fuse nicely, too. However, some synthetics and metallic fibers are too heat sensitive for fusible interfacings.

Textured fabrics, such as tweeds and linen weaves, tailor well; their surfaces give the fusible adhesive something to grip for a strong bond. On the other hand, some fabrics with tight weaves and smooth surfaces, such as fine polyester gabardines, resist smooth fusing and should be used with sew-in interfacing.

Preshrink tailoring fabrics to prepare them for the extra steam used when fusing interfacings and to prevent shrinkage of the garment. Thorough steam-pressing preshrinks fabric effectively without sacrificing the fresh, new look. Steam-press fabric at home, or have a drycleaner do it for you. A faster and easier preshrinking method is tossing the fabric into a clothes dryer with a few damp towels. Tumble for 7 to 10 minutes at a medium-high heat. Remove immediately; lay flat to dry. Steam-press if necessary.

Sequence for Tailoring a Jacket

The first step in tailoring a jacket is to fuse interfacing onto the major sections. Make pockets next. Then sew the jacket together and make a notched or shawl collar. Finish the sleeves, including the sleeve hems, and set them in. Shape the shoulders with shoulder pads and sleeve heads. Hem the jacket, and sew the lining as the final step.

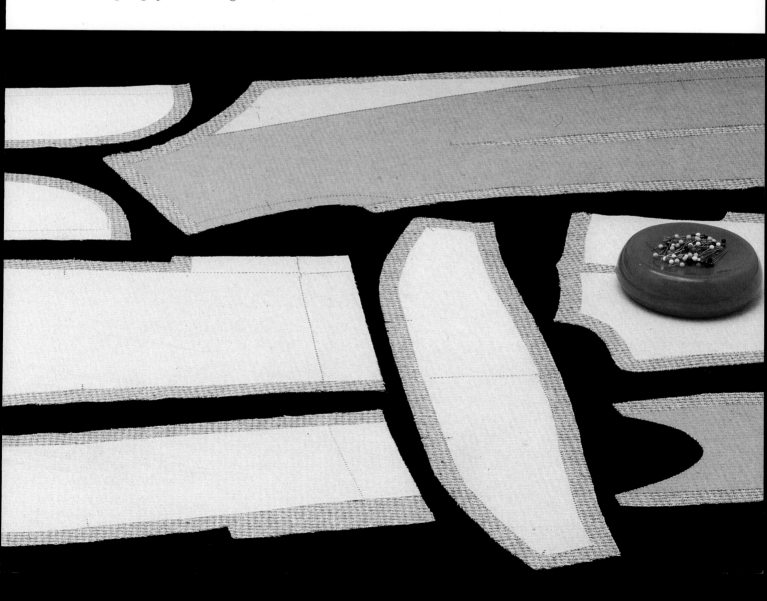

Interfacing the Jacket Sections

In one session, fuse interfacing to the jacket front, facing, back, collar, undercollar, and sleeves. Grouping the work is an efficient way to prepare major jacket sections for the steps that follow. After fusing, let the sections cool and dry on a flat surface. Wait overnight before handling medium to heavyweight woolens and textured tweeds. Wait one or two hours for fabrics of lighter weight.

Fusible interfacing is cut on the seamline rather than the cutting line in all places except at the armhole. Stitch interfacing in the seam at the armhole to support the sleeve. For lightweight fabrics, use the cutting line at the hem instead of the hem foldline.

How to Interface a Jacket Front and Facing

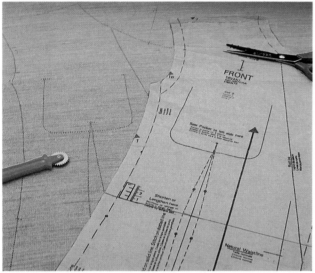

1) Trace seamlines of jacket front and side front pattern pieces on fusible weft insertion or hair canvas. Transfer all pattern markings to interfacing, including lapel roll line and dart stitching lines; it is unnecessary to mark fashion fabric.

2) Cut out any darts on dart stitching lines to eliminate bulk. Dart in fashion fabric will be stitched along cut edge of interfacing.

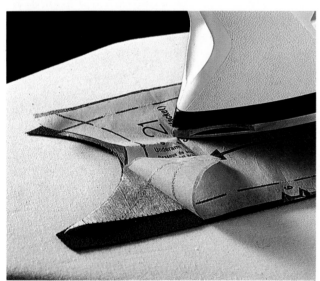

3) Place interfacing, adhesive side down, on wrong side of jacket sections. Place pattern on top to position darts and edges of interfacing at seamlines. Using dry iron, tack interfacing in place to prepare for permanent fusing. Set pattern piece aside.

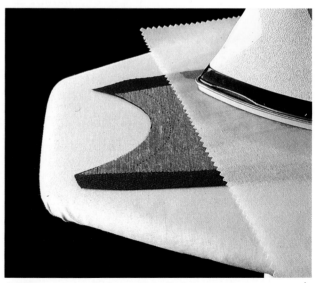

4) Place press cloth on interfacing. Begin at center of section, then fuse each end. To avoid disturbing fused sections, fuse remaining areas by alternating from one side to the other. Never slide iron, which could cause layers to shift.

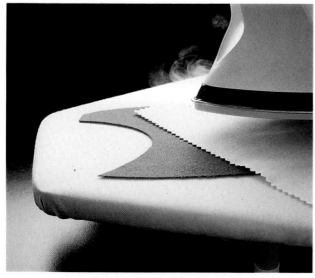

5) Turn jacket section over to right side. Using dry press cloth to protect right side of fabric, press thoroughly with steam iron. Lay flat to allow fused sections to cool and dry completely.

6) Fuse tricot knit interfacing or lightweight nonwoven interfacing to front facings after trimming seam allowances at front of facings. Interfacing extends to outer edge of facing.

Shaping Lapels

Layer. Add second layer of interfacing to lapel area only. Use weft insertion fusible interfacing, and cut it to fit from roll line to seamline of lapel; roll line should be placed on straight grain of interfacing to stabilize bias grain of jacket at roll line.

Hinge. When using fusible hair canvas, use a hinged roll line for a sharper edge on bulky or heavyweight fabrics. To make a hinge, cut interfacing on lapel roll line before fusing interfacing to jacket front.

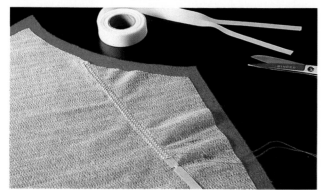

Tape. Use narrow twill tape ¼" to ½" (6 mm to 1.3 cm) shorter than lapel roll line to contour roll line; shorten tape ½" (1.3 cm) for full bust. Place one edge of tape next to roll line; zigzag both tape edges to jacket, easing interfacing to fit tape.

Fold fused lapel on roll line, and press a crease. Do not press crease at lower 2" (5 cm) of lapel roll line; gently steam this area instead. Lay lapel over tailor's ham for pressing. Leave lapel on ham until lapel is completely cool and dry.

How to Interface a Jacket Back with Fusible Interfacing

1) Cut interfacing for jacket back from same interfacing used for jacket front, or use lighter weight interfacing. Cut and mark as for jacket front interfacing, page 78, steps 1 and 2.

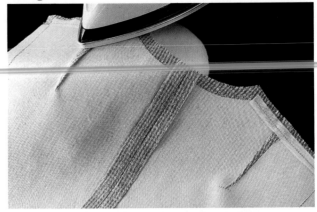

2) Fuse interfacing to jacket back, using same technique as for interfacing jacket front, pages 78 and 79, steps 3 to 5. Fuse interfacing to both jacket back sections before stitching center back seam.

How to Interface a Jacket Back and Hem

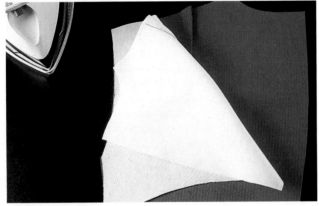

1) Cut partial jacket back interfacing from lightweight woven fabric when garment does not need a fused interfacing for the entire back. Stitch darts separately in interfacing and garment. Press interfacing darts toward armhole and garment darts toward center back.

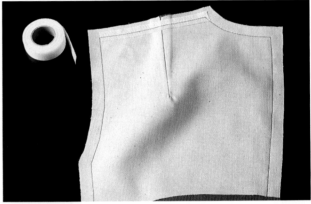

2) Staystitch interfacing to jacket back, ½" (1.3 cm) from raw edges. Include narrow twill tape stay in staystitching at shoulders to prevent bias shoulder seam from stretching.

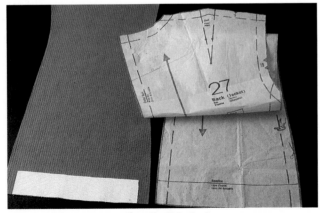

Hem without vent. Cut fusible knit or nonwoven interfacing crosswise to fit shape of hem from hem fold to raw edge; cut fusible weft insertion on the bias. Fuse as for jacket front interfacing, pages 78 and 79, steps 3 to 6.

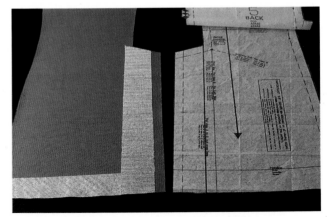

Hem with vent. Cut interfacing to stabilize vent underlap and overlap. Place straight grain of interfacing on lap foldlines.

How to Interface and Shape a Jacket Undercollar

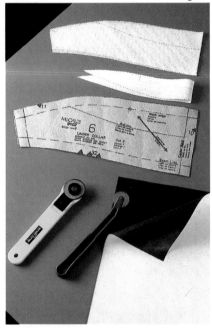

1) Cut undercollar from fusible weft insertion or hair canvas on bias grain. To cut collar stand interfacing, trace undercollar pattern from roll line to neckline seam; place center back seam on straight grain fold.

2) Transfer all pattern markings to both layers of interfacing. Fuse interfacing to undercollar; stitch center back seam. Fuse stand after stitching seam.

3) Fold undercollar on roll line, and press a sharp crease. Pin as pressed around tailor's ham, and steam. Leave in place on ham until completely cool and dry.

How to Interface Sleeves

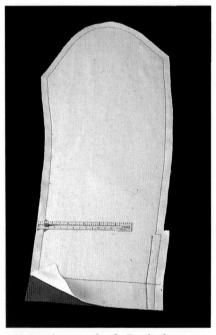

1) Use lightweight fusible interfacing for comfort and appearance. Cut interfacing on seamlines of sleeve pattern. At sleeve hem, use cutting line instead of seamline. Transfer all pattern markings to sleeve interfacing.

2) Fuse interfacing to sleeve sections before sewing seams.

Alternative method: Back the jacket sleeves with batiste. Transfer pattern markings to batiste. Staystitch batiste to sleeve, ½" (1.3 cm) from raw edges. Machine-baste along hem and vent foldlines.

Tailoring a Notched Collar

A notched collar takes its name from the angle of the jacket collar where it joins the jacket lapels. The seams that meet there form a *notch,* or V-shaped cutout, on each side of the neckline. The seam is the *gorge* line. A crisp, flat, even notch is a hallmark of fine tailoring. The key to this detail is an artful combination of stitching and pressing, plus careful trimming of enclosed seam allowances to reduce bulk.

Several pattern pieces are needed to make a notched collar. The undercollar, interfaced and shaped, is the first section to be sewn to the jacket. Next, sew the upper collar to the facing; a portion of this facing becomes the outside of the lapels when the collar is finished. After sewing the final seam, which attaches the collar/facing section to the jacket, press and edgestitch or topstitch, using techniques on page 87 to shape and stitch the notches.

Tailoring a Shawl Collar

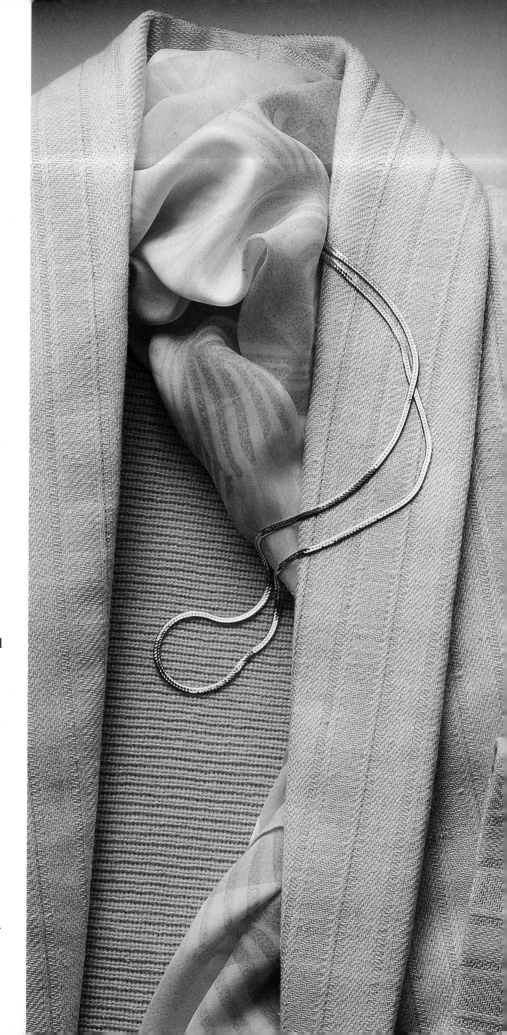

A shawl collar is shaped in a continuous tapering line with no distinction between the collar and lapels. It is often used with double-breasted patterns or with belted wrap styles. Because a shawl collar requires fewer pattern pieces, it is usually easier to tailor than a notched collar. The shawl collar is cut as one section, which includes the jacket lapels. A single, center back collar seam shows on the outside of the collar. This streamlines stitching, trimming, and pressing in the neckline area.

Some of the steps for tailoring a shawl collar are the same as for tailoring a notched collar; the only difference is the shape of the pattern pieces. Before tailoring a shawl collar, interface the jacket front, back, and sleeves; interface and shape the undercollar; shape the lapels, and press the lapel roll line as for a tailored notched collar (pages 84 to 87).

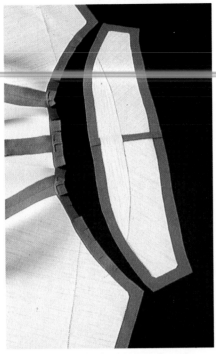

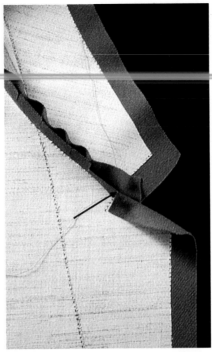

1) Staystitch jacket ½" (1.3 cm) from neckline raw edge. Clip to staystitching. This releases curved neckline seam allowance so it lies flat for easier sewing.

2) Match pattern markings to line up undercollar and jacket neckline edge. Stitch undercollar to jacket neckline up to pattern markings on lapels (arrow); clip to marking.

3) Press seam open over tailor's ham. Trim seam allowances to ¼" (6 mm) to reduce bulk.

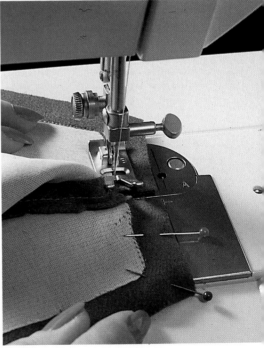

7) Trim excess fabric of collar seam allowance to stitching line on upper and undercollar.

8) Stitch seam, starting at bottom of one jacket edge. Shorten stitches 1" (2.5 cm) from lapel. Take one or two short stitches diagonally across lapel point. (Lapel removed from machine to show stitching.)

9) Stitch from lapel point to collar point, holding seam straight to ensure that notches match on both sides of jacket collar. Finish stitching seam, using same technique on other side.

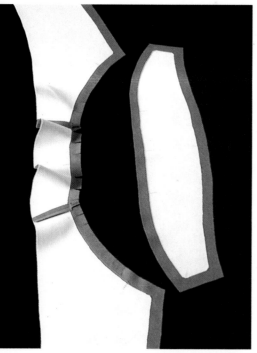

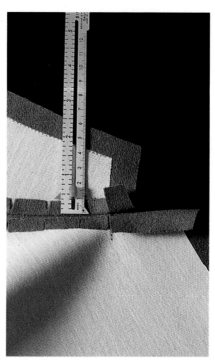

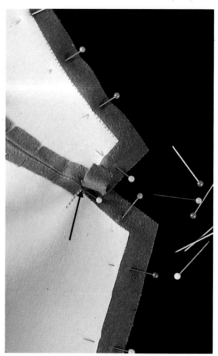

4) Staystitch facing ½" (1.3 cm) from neckline edge. Clip to staystitching. Stitch collar to facing neckline up to pattern markings on lapels; clip to marking.

5) Press seam open over tailor's ham. Trim seam allowances to ⅜" (1 cm), slightly wider than undercollar to reduce bulk.

6) Pin collar/facing section to undercollar/jacket section, pinning through seams at collar notches (arrow) to be sure the seams line up precisely.

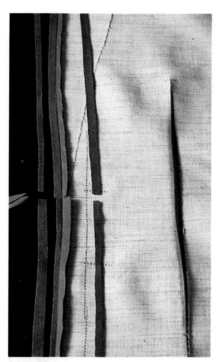

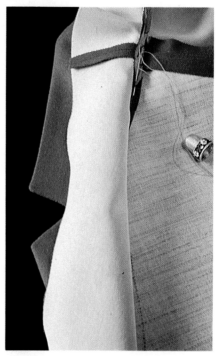

10) Press seam open, using point presser at lapel and collar points. Diagonally trim corners close to stitching. Grade seam allowance on undercollar/lapel to ¼" (6 mm), and on collar/facing to ⅜" (1 cm). Continue grading to lapel roll line.

11) Clip seam at ends of lapel roll line. Below clips, grade jacket front seam allowance to ⅜" (1 cm) and facing to ¼" (6 mm). Press seam open, turn right side out.

12) Tack upper and undercollar seams together with loose running stitch. If seams do not line up exactly because of bulk of fabric, tack the seams where they meet.

How to Sew a Tailored Shawl Collar

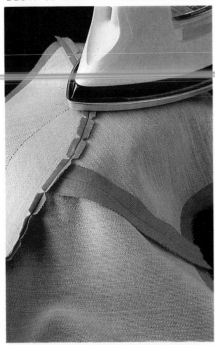

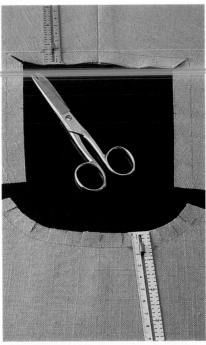

1) Stitch undercollar to jacket as for notched collar, page 84, steps 1 to 3. Cut out tiny notches so undercollar seam allowance lies flat at lapels. Press seam open.

2) Staystitch collar neck edge on seamline, using small reinforcement stitches at corners. Clip to stitching at corners. Staystitch back facing ½" (1.3 cm) from neckline; clip.

3) Pin and stitch facing to collar. At corners of collar neck seamline, spread clips and stitch seam straight across corners.

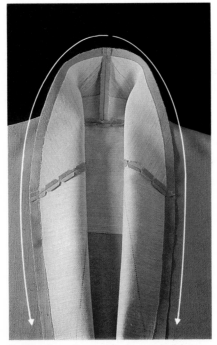

4) Cut square from collar seam allowance at each corner. Trim seam allowances to ⅜" (1 cm). Press seam open over tailor's ham.

5) Stitch collar to jacket, stitching directionally. Begin at center back. Directional stitching prevents distorted, puckered seams on bias grain at collar edges. Trim and finish as for notched collar, page 85, step 12.

6) Understitch outer edge of collar and lapels with undercollar and garment side up. End stitching about 1" (2.5 cm) above roll line. Or topstitch instead, following instructions opposite.

Tips for Pressing a Tailored Collar

 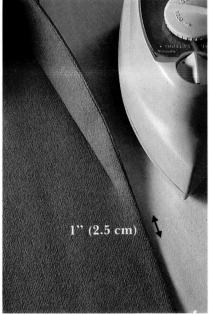 

1) Press collar and lapels from underside. Roll seam toward underside of collar and lapels, stopping about 1" (2.5 cm) from end of lapel roll line. Press, using tailor's clapper to force steam out of fabric; this creates crisp edge.

2) Press lower 1" (2.5 cm) of lapel roll line so seam is at edge. Work from underside of lapels.

3) Press jacket front below lapel roll line from inside. Press so seam rolls toward jacket facing.

How to Topstitch a Tailored Collar

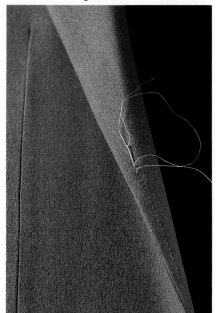  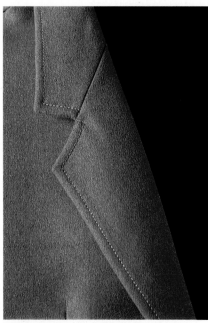

1) Topstitch on right side of jacket, beginning at one lower edge. When using topstitching thread in the needle, stop at bottom of lapel roll line. Clip threads. Pull threads through to facing side; bury ends between facing and garment.

2) Continue topstitching from right side of lapel. Start at exact point where stitching ended, or overlap 2 stitches. At collar notch, pivot and stitch up to notch edge. (The garment is off the machine only to show detail. Do not remove from machine.)

3) Shorten stitch length, pivot, and stitch in the ditch to topstitching line of collar. Pivot, and stitch around collar to other notch. Repeat at second notch. Break topstitching at end of lapel roll line as described in step 1.

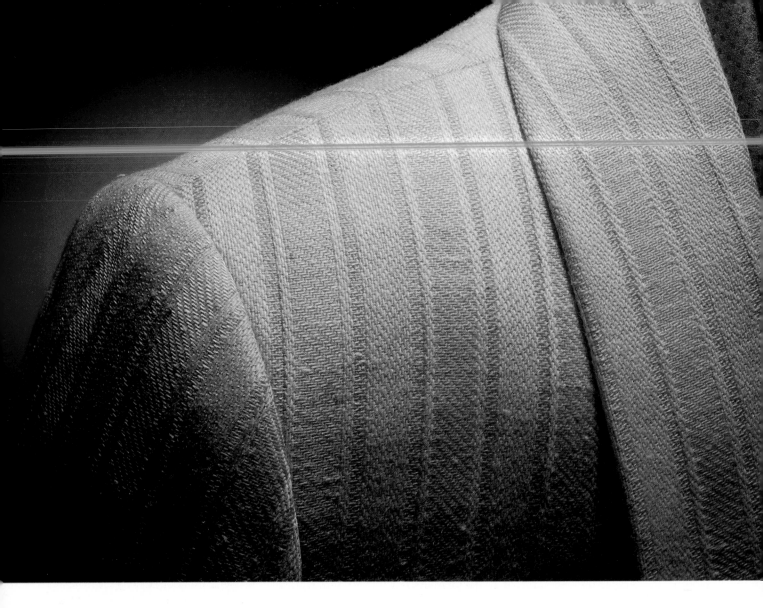

Shaping the Shoulders

Jackets need inside support for firm, smooth shape at the shoulders. In tailoring, the two important shaping aids are shoulder pads and sleeve heads.

Shoulder pads can be custom-made to fit the jacket armhole, using the jacket pattern pieces. To fit your figure, adjust the size and thickness of the shoulder pad. If one shoulder is higher than the other one, the pad can be made thicker to compensate for the difference. If your shoulders are sloping, use a thicker pad than the pattern suggests. For square shoulders, use a thinner shoulder pad.

On tailored garments such as jackets and coats, the front of the shoulder pad is wider than the back to fill in the hollow area below the shoulder and to create a smooth line. The back is narrower than the front to fit around the shoulder blades. For a full bust, make the shoulder pad slightly shorter in front. Whenever you try on the jacket or coat for fitting, slip the shoulder pads in place. The shape

and size of the shoulder pads can make a big difference in the way the shoulder and sleeve fit.

To build the pads to the desired thickness, cut graduated layers of a thin filler, such as polyester fleece or cotton/polyester quilt batting. These fillers add lift without being too soft. For the upper layer of a shoulder pad, use fusible hair canvas. The goat's hair fibers in the canvas grip the jacket fabric, helping to secure the pad to the garment. Also, the strong, resilient canvas makes the shoulder pads firm and wrinkle free.

Sleeve heads are strips of filler that support the sleeve caps on a tailored jacket to boost the caps and smooth out any wrinkles where the sleeve was eased to fit the armhole. Sleeve heads also improve the way the jacket sleeves drape. The same filler used for shoulder pads (fleece or quilt batting) can be used to make sleeve heads. Necktie interfacing cut on the true bias grain can also be used.

How to Make a Custom Shoulder Pad

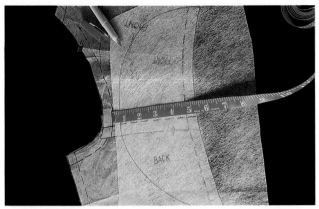

1) Lap jacket front and back patterns at shoulder seam. Trace armhole between front and back notches. End shoulder pad pattern ½" (1.3 cm) from neck seam edge, about 5" (12.5 cm) from armhole. Mark shoulder seam on pad pattern. Label armhole front and armhole back.

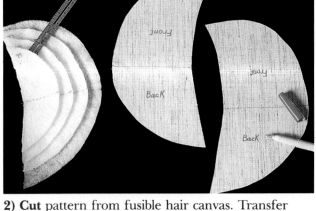

2) Cut pattern from fusible hair canvas. Transfer shoulder seam markings. Mark front and back of armhole on canvas. Also cut four layers of filler, gradually reducing layers by about ¾" (2 cm) in size, to make ½" (1.3 cm) thick pad. Adjust sizes and numbers of layers to make pad desired thickness.

3) Stitch around armhole edge and across shoulder marking with running stitches to hold filler layers together. Add more rows of stitches about 1" (2.5 cm) apart, fanning rows out from armhole edge.

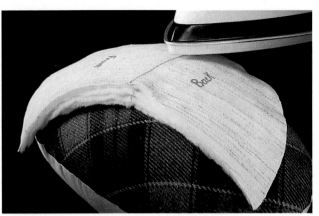

4) Fuse hair canvas to widest layer of fleece, placing pad over tailor's ham to press pad to shape of shoulder. Tack pad to jacket by hand as shown on page 55, placing canvas layer next to jacket.

How to Make a Sleeve Head

1) Cut strip of filler 1⅞" (4.7 cm) deep and the length of jacket sleeve cap. Sleeve cap is eased area of set-in sleeve, between pattern markings. Match one long edge of sleeve head to raw edge of armhole seam allowance.

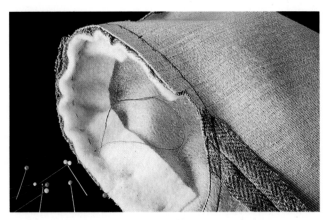

2) Stitch sleeve head to seamline around sleeve cap, using running stitches. When sleeve is turned right side out, sleeve head folds into two layers. Top layer extends beyond bottom layer to prevent ridge on outside of jacket.

Tailored Hems

Tailored hems on jackets and jacket sleeves are best put in with a catchstitch. These are small horizontal stitches made in a zigzag pattern. With a blind catchstitch, the stitches do not show from the inside or the outside of the jacket because they are worked between the hem edge and the jacket or sleeve. The hem is not held tightly against the garment; it should be sewn loosely with some play at the raw edge. A tailored hem should not show a ridge on the outside of the jacket after pressing, even if a bulky fabric is used.

Determine hem lengths on jackets and sleeves before cutting out the pattern pieces. Although the depth can vary, the standard hem on a jacket is 2" (5 cm) deep. The standard sleeve hem is 1½" (3.8 cm) deep. Hem a jacket after completing the collar or before sewing in the lining. For easier handling, sew sleeve hems before setting the sleeves into the jacket.

Trimming. Trim seam allowances within the hem to half their width, from raw edge of hem to hemline only. This reduces bulk and prevents bumps where seams cross hemline.

Edge finishing. Lining covers the hem edge when a jacket is completed, so finishing this edge may not be necessary. Finish the edge only if the fabric ravels or stretches. Use a nonbulky zigzagged, overlocked, or stitched-and-pinked finish. If you have fused the interfacing, the edge is stabilized adequately and needs no further finishing.

Pressing. Press the hem before sewing. If a jacket hem is very curved, use a line of easestitching along the raw hem edge to help ease in fabric fullness.

How to Sew a Tailored Hem

1) Turn hem up and press at hem foldline. Open out pressed hem and trim seam allowances to half width from raw edge of hem to foldline. Baste hem in place close to fold.

2) Press, letting steam penetrate fabric to ease extra fullness in smoothly. To avoid a ridge on right side, do not press over upper edge of hem.

Catchstitch for lined garments. Work loosely over hem edge from left to right. Make stitch in hem, catching one or two threads; then make a stitch just outside hem edge, catching a single thread of garment. Alternate stitches in zigzag pattern.

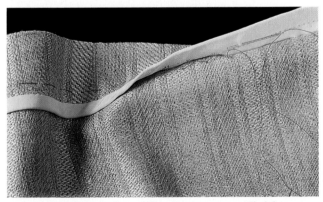

Blind catchstitch for unlined garments. Finish raw edge with appropriate edge finish. Baste hem in place close to finished edge. Fold hem edge down and loosely catchstitch between hem and garment. Stitching is not visible.

How to Hem a Jacket Vent

1) Arrange vent in finished position. Clip seam so underlap lies flat. From inside of jacket, vent underlap is on top with seam allowance pressed back; overlap on bottom has self-facing folded back.

2) Press hem into position on overlap. Press fold at hem and at vent self-facing to prepare for mitering. Clip vent facing and hem allowance where two edges meet.

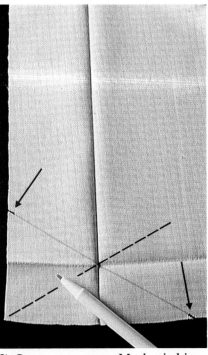

3) Open out corner. Mark stitching line from clips (arrows) through corner point where pressed lines meet. Fold through corner (dotted line), with right sides together, matching clip marks.

4) Stitch on marked line. Trim seam to ¼" (6 mm). Press seam open; turn to right side.

5) Fold hem to outside on vent underlap, right sides together. Stitch seam from hem fold to top of hem. Trim to ¼" (6 mm) and press open; turn right side out. Catchstitch hem and vent in place.

6) Arrange vent in finished position. Stitch across top of vent from inside through all layers. Grade seam.

Linings

Linings hide the inside construction, covering raw edges, interfacing, and the wrong side of the fabric. When tailored jackets have welt pockets and shoulder shaping aids as well as interfacings, linings are especially important for a neat, finished look.

A lining adds to the life of a garment by making the garment stronger. On jackets the lining takes the wear and strain at underarms, across the shoulders, and at the elbows. On skirts the lining prevents the seat from stretching and becoming baggy. On pants the lining protects the outer fabric at knees, seat, and crotch seam. A lining in skirts and pants allows you to use open-weave, lightweight, or fragile fabrics that could not be used otherwise.

Lined garments are also more comfortable to wear. Jackets, even when worn over sweaters, slip on and off more easily if lined. A lined skirt can be worn without a slip. Pants can be made from light colors and white fabrics which would be too revealing unless lined. A lining fabric makes it possible to wear fabrics that may cause allergic reactions.

Choosing Lining Fabrics

Many different fabrics can be used for linings as long as they are smooth so the garment slides on and off easily. It's also important that a lining fabric be finely woven or knitted so it is durable, opaque in jackets and coats so inside construction does not show through, and lighter in weight than the fashion fabric so it does not add bulk.

Fabrics made especially for linings are often treated to resist static, wrinkles, fading, and perspiration damage. Linings are available in fabric types such as taffeta, twill weaves, jacquard weaves, crepe-back satin, sateen, tricot, and batiste. Typical fibers are

acetate, polyester, and nylon or fiber blends. China silk is a very lightweight lining made from pure silk fibers, as its name implies.

Silky blouse and dress fabrics can often be used for linings. These dressmaking fabrics come in a wide selection of prints and stripes, as well as fashion colors. Use them to make linings decorative as well as practical. You can also use them for ensembles with a custom look, matching the jacket lining to a blouse or dress.

Select a lining color that matches the outer fabric, or choose a contrasting color if you prefer. Layer outer fabric and lining fabric before you buy to make sure that a dark color or pattern does not show through to the right side.

Most lining fabrics are washable and can be machine-washed and machine-dried to preshrink. To preserve the new look of the lining, thoroughly steam-press it instead. Test a scrap first to be sure that steam does not damage or spot the fabric.

Tips for Handling Lining Fabrics

Practically all linings have a shine or sheen on the right side. This requires a "with nap" cutting layout with all the lining pattern pieces placed in the same direction. This treatment keeps the color shading uniform in the finished lining.

Lining fabrics can be slippery to handle. Cut with the fabric folded wrong sides together to minimize slipping. Cover the cutting surface with a bed sheet to help control very slippery lining fabrics. Cut lining fabrics with sharp shears or rotary cutter. Shears with serrated blades help grip the fabric. Dull blades will chew the fabric and fray the raw edges.

Lining a Jacket

A lining is cut and sewn along the same style lines as a jacket, but has extra details designed to add comfort. A pleat in the center back of the lining allows for wearing ease across shoulders and upper back. A pleat also is formed between the lining and hems. This is a *jump hem,* and it allows you to move comfortably while wearing the jacket without straining the stitches to the breaking point.

Some jacket patterns provide separate pattern pieces for the lining, and others furnish cutting lines for the lining on the jacket pattern itself. If the same pattern is used for the sleeve and the sleeve lining, cut the sleeve lining ½" (1.3 cm) higher at the underarms. This allows the lining to rest above the jacket underarm seams and prevents binding at the armholes. When a separate sleeve lining pattern is provided, this may have been done for you. Check by placing the sleeve and sleeve lining pattern pieces with one on top of the other, matching the underarm seamlines.

Cut the jacket and sleeve lining ½" (1.3 cm) longer than the finished length after hemming. After the lining is applied to jacket and sleeve hems, the finished edges of the lining will fall just below the halfway point on the jacket and sleeve hems. If you shortened or lengthened the jacket or sleeves, make the same adjustments on the lining pattern pieces.

How to Line a Jacket

  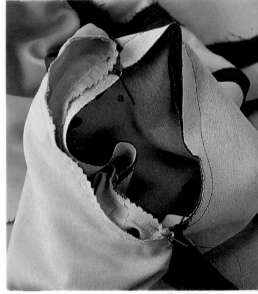

1) Stitch lining sections together, including sleeves. Reinforce armhole seam with two rows of stitching. Fold and machine-baste center back pleat at top and bottom of lining. Staystitch ½" (1.3 cm) from neckline, sleeve, and lower edges of lining; clip to staystitching at neckline.

2) Turn jacket facing out. With right sides together, stitch lining to facing. On each side in front, leave seam unstitched for twice the depth of hem. [Leave 4" (10 cm) unstitched if jacket hem is 2" (5 cm) deep.] Clip seam allowance at curves. Press seam as stitched.

3) Match seam allowances of lining and jacket at shoulder **(a)** and underarm **(b)** seams; tack in place. Turn lining right side out. Smooth sleeves into position on inside of jacket. Lightly press facing/lining seam allowances toward lining, using a press cloth.

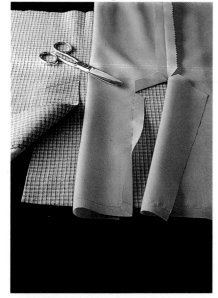

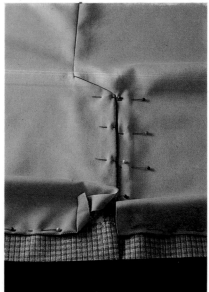

1) Stitch center back seam to marking at top of vent; clip into seam so left side of vent lies flat. Staystitch right side of vent on seamline across top and on foldline. Clip into corner to fold under raw edge on staystitching. Attach lining to jacket facing, following steps 1 to 3, below.

2) Match center back seams of lining and jacket at vent opening. Fold under ⅝" (1.5 cm) seam allowance across top of left vent lining and down side. Pin lining to side edges of vent on jacket; leave top edge unpinned. Match raw edge of lining to jacket hem edge, forming pleat at bottom of vent.

3) Sew lining to hems, following steps 4 and 5, below. Slipstitch vent lining along vent side edges. Stitch across top of vent lining. To prevent lining from pulling at top of vent, slipstitches should not go through to jacket fabric.

4) Trim raw edges of front facing to neaten them, if necessary. Whipstitch raw edges to hem. Turn lining under on staystitching line at lower edge. Pin so raw edge of lining is even with top edge of jacket hem.

5) Slipstitch lining fold to jacket hem, sewing through jacket hem allowance only. At front edges, fold lining hem down to form pleat, and slipstitch to facing on each side.

6) Sew lining to each sleeve hem, following steps 4 and 5. Sew jump hem around entire sleeve, even if sleeve hem has vent; sleeve vents are decorative and not meant to open and close. Press sleeve lining hem over seam roll.

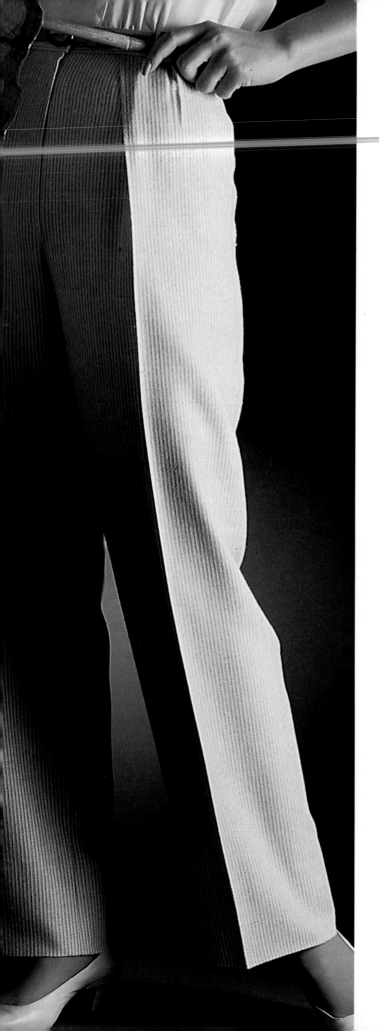

Lining Skirts & Pants

Few patterns provide linings for skirts and pants, but adding a lining makes garments hang better and is easy to accomplish. The method given here is for a slip lining, which is free-hanging and attached at the waistline; the skirt or pants and the lining are hemmed separately. An advantage of a slip lining is that the garment is easy to press because you can lift the whole lining out.

Unlike jacket and coat linings, skirt and pants linings are usually worn next to your skin. In warm or humid climates, fabrics made from rayon, cotton, or cotton blends may feel more comfortable than those made from polyester and similar synthetic fibers.

Tips for Lining Skirts & Pants

Cut the lining from the major front and back pattern pieces. Omit small pattern pieces such as the waistband, facings, and pockets. For a gathered skirt in a lightweight fabric, the skirt and lining may be treated as one layer of fabric. For a heavier weight gathered skirt, cut the lining from a pattern for a simple A-line skirt, or make small pleats or released tucks instead of gathers in the lining. Or pleat out the fullness from the tissue pattern before cutting the lining, allowing some ease for movement. Any of these methods eliminates bulk at the waistline.

Omit any seam extensions for in-seam pockets when you cut out a lining. Straighten the cutting lines on the front and back pattern pieces to change the pocket openings to plain seams. If the garment has slanted pockets, lap the front pattern pieces to cut the lining without pockets.

Shorten the pattern pieces so the lining will be 1" (2.5 cm) shorter than the skirt or pants after hemming. If you plan to make a 1" (2.5 cm) hem in the lining, cut the lower edge of the lining at the hemline of the skirt or pants.

Transfer pattern markings at the zipper opening and the waist to the lining sections after cutting. These markings will help you position the lining inside the skirt or pants.

Assemble the skirt or pants, including the zipper and pockets, before attaching the lining. All stitching on the garment should be completed except for the waistband and the hem. Press seams open. Unless the fabric ravels easily, it is not necessary to finish the seams.

How to Line a Skirt

1) Stitch lining seams, leaving seam open at zipper; press open. Slip lining over skirt, wrong sides together, matching seams. Machine-baste together on waist seamline, folding lining under at zipper edge.

2) Fold lining edges under to expose zipper coil and allow easy opening and closing of zipper. Pin and slipstitch lining to zipper tape.

3) Apply waistband. Hem lining so it is 1" (2.5 cm) shorter than skirt. Sew lining hem by hand or machine, as desired.

Darts, Ease, or Pleats in Linings

Darts. Pin tucks in the skirt or pants lining, matching the dart markings. Darts in skirt or pants are pressed toward center front and back. Press tucks in lining in opposite direction to reduce bulk.

Eased or slightly gathered area. Slip lining over skirt, wrong sides together. Machine-baste at waistline seam. Gather lining and skirt as if they were one layer of fabric, pulling up ease to fit waistband.

Pleat-front skirts or pants. Machine-baste pleats separately in lining and garment. Press lining pleats flat in opposite direction of skirt pleats. Slip lining over skirt, wrong sides together. Machine-baste at waistline.

How to Line a Skirt with a Kick Pleat

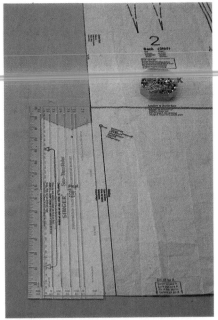

1) Cut lining from skirt pattern, eliminating pleat extension. Add ⅝" (1.5 cm) seam allowance at foldline of pleat. Stitch lining seams. Leave lining seam unstitched below top of pleat and at zipper opening. Clip seam allowance at each end of stitching.

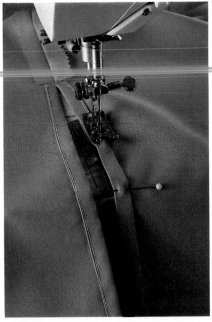

2) Press under ⅝" (1.5 cm) seam allowance at pleat opening. Turn under ¼" (6 mm) to form a narrow ⅜" (1 cm) hem. Edgestitch folded hem. Finish opening at zipper in the same way.

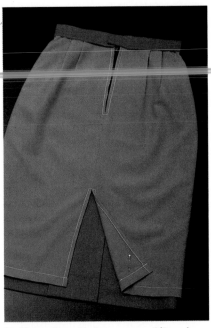

3) Complete lining, page 97, using method that applies to waistline details. Do not attach lining at zipper opening or pleat. For walking ease, lining forms slit at pleat.

How to Line a Skirt with a Hem Slit

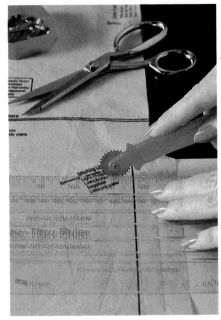

1) Cut partial skirt lining so lower edge of lining falls above slit in skirt hem. Allow ¼" (6 mm) to finish lower edge of lining. Stitch lining seams, leaving lining seam open in zipper area.

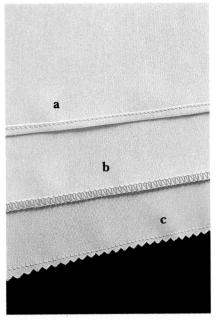

2) Finish lower edge of the lining with flat finish such as **(a)** turned-and-stitched, **(b)** serged, or **(c)** stitched-and-pinked edge. Pink, serge, or zigzag lining seams to prevent raveling.

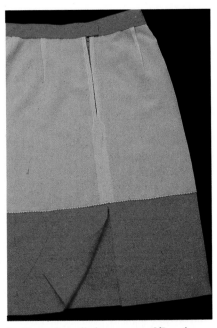

3) Complete lining, page 97, using method that applies to waistline details. Partial lining will not show at slit when skirt is finished.

How to Line Pants with a Fly-front Closing

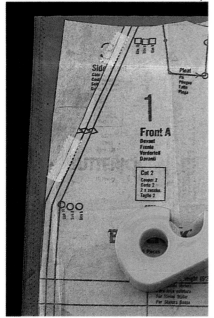

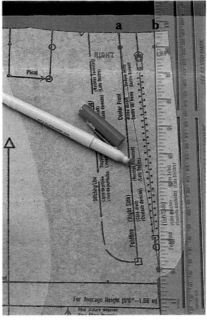

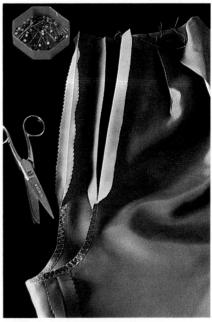

1) Omit slanted pockets by lapping pattern pieces for side front pocket and pants front. Cut front lining on pocket cutting line.

2) Mark ⅝" (1.5 cm) on each side of zipper placement at waist seamline. Mark diagonal lines from these two points to bottom of fly front. Cut on inside diagonal line **(a)** for right side; cut on outside diagonal line **(b)** for left side. (In linings, left and right are reversed.)

3) Cut lining; stitch seams, darts, or pleats. Leave seam open at fly-front closing. Reinforce crotch seam with stretch stitch or two rows of stitching between notches. Trim seam to ¼" (6 mm), and zigzag edges together. Press under ⅝" (1.5 cm) seam allowances above crotch reinforcement stitching.

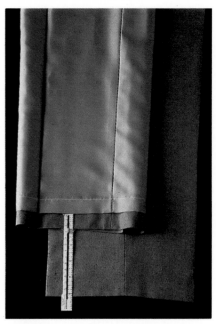

4) Turn under ¼" (6 mm) to form narrow ⅜" (1 cm) hem on each side of zipper opening. Edgestitch folded hem.

5) Slip lining over pants, wrong sides together. Machine-baste pants and lining together on waist seamline, matching seams, darts, and waistband markings. Leave lining free, or tack to zipper as desired.

6) Hem pants. Hem lining 1" (2.5 cm) shorter than pants. Leave lining free, or tack to side seams as desired.

Distinctive Details

Distinctive Details

Distinctive details are the extras that you add to a garment to make it special. They offer a way for you to put a personal stamp on mass-produced pattern designs, and they give a look of quality and style to the garments you sew.

The fashion appearance of a classic style can change entirely according to the details used. For example, jackets and dresses made from the same commercial pattern can achieve an individual look with the addition of binding, jewel trim, or ribbon weaving.

Some of the distinctive details featured on the following pages are shortcuts and can be completed quickly; others require an investment of time. The emphasis throughout is not on complicated sewing, but rather on imagination and originality. You can adapt the methods to specific projects in your own way and with your choice of materials.

Creative edge finishes are alternatives to traditional hems and facings. These designer treatments are especially attractive on classic garments but can be adapted for many other styles.

Decorative seams are made with nontraditional sewing methods. Seam allowances and stitches normally hidden inside garments are displayed on the outside as textured self-trims. Use these seams for an entire garment, or use them sparingly for accent.

Unique embellishments require special application techniques, but your sewing time can save you money. Custom-decorated garments command high prices, whether the decoration is sequins, cutwork, or machine appliqué.

Creative Edge Finishes

Give a designer touch to garments by taking a fresh look at the edges. Instead of conventional hems and facings, add decorative accents such as synthetic suede binding, a contrasting fabric band, or a mock bound hem that looks like a binding. Other alternatives include crocheted edgings, piping, and fringe. Finish inside facing edges with a lining of fusible interfacing for a ravel-free finish.

Bindings

Cut your own binding from nonraveling synthetic suede to trim a garment with a neat, elegant edging. The application is similar to the Hong Kong method used to bind inside raw edges of seams or hems with a lightweight fabric. Suede binding can be used on many fabrics but is especially suitable for bulky fabrics because facings can be eliminated. Also use it to finish edges of double-faced fabrics or garments that are lined to the edge.

Contrasting banding is suitable for garments of most fabric weights, but to avoid bulkiness, do not use heavy fabric for the banding. The banding method is similar to binding an edge with suede, but the contrasting bands are cut on the bias and finished by hand with slipstitching. Cut bands from a fabric contrasting in texture and luster with the garment fabric. For example, trim a tweed or nubby fabric with bands cut from wool flannel, lightweight gabardine, or wool crepe.

A contrasting band is often featured on the front closing of a jacket. To prepare the edge for band finishing, baste the facing to the jacket, wrong sides together. The completed band encloses the raw edges of the jacket and the facing. To further enhance this trim, insert piping in the seams, or cover the seams with one or more flat braid trims.

How to Bind an Edge with Synthetic Suede

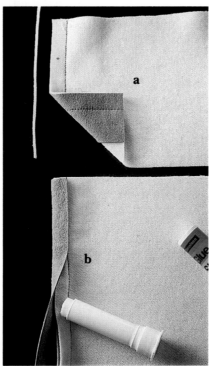

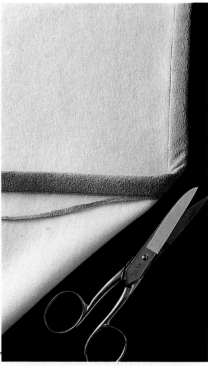

1) Cut suede strips three times the desired finished width of binding, plus ¼" (6 mm). Pin binding to garment, right sides together, with one width of binding in seam allowance. Stitch on seamline.

2) Trim raw edge of garment even with edge of binding **(a)**. Fold binding over raw edge to wrong side of garment. Use glue stick to hold binding in place **(b)**.

3) Stitch in the ditch at edge of binding, working from right side of garment. On wrong side, trim binding close to stitching.

How to Finish an Edge with a Contrasting Band

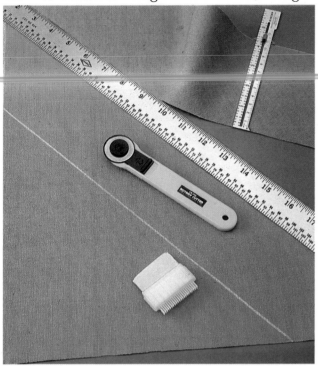

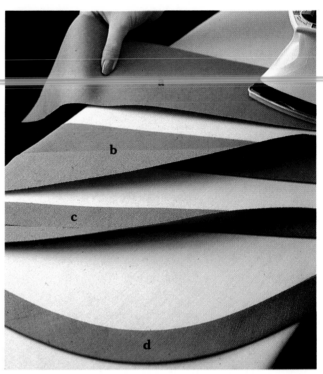

1) Cut band of contrasting fabric four times desired finished width plus ¼" to ⅜" (6 mm to 1 cm). Finished width can be as great as 1" (2.5 cm) or as narrow as ¼" (6 mm). Cut band on true bias grain.

2) Preshape binding. Steam-press and stretch slightly to take out slack **(a)**. Fold strip in half lengthwise, wrong sides together; press **(b)**. Open binding, and fold cut edges toward center; press **(c)**. Shape tape into curves that match garment **(d)**.

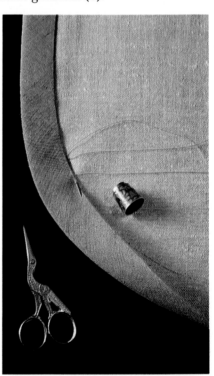

3) Trim seam allowances from garment edge. Pin band to garment, right sides together. Miter any corners as shown for synthetic suede binding, opposite.

4) Stitch band to garment, using seam allowance equal to desired finished width of band. Stitch carefully so completed band will be uniformly wide.

5) Press band away from garment. On inside of garment, turn under raw edge of band so fold covers seam. Slipstitch fold to garment, and press.

How to Miter a Corner with Synthetic Suede Binding

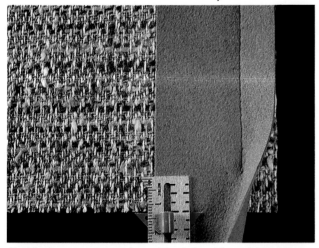

1) Stitch toward corner, with right sides of binding and garment together. Stop a distance from corner equal to desired finished width of binding.

2) Fold binding on diagonal, away from garment. Clip the binding to mark a distance from the seam equal to the desired finished width of binding.

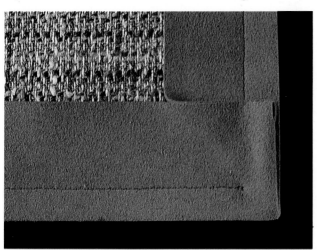

3) Fold binding at mark to turn corner. Resume stitching to apply binding to garment edge.

4) Fold binding over raw edge to wrong side of garment. Mitered fold forms in binding at corner on right side of garment.

5) Fold binding into mitered fold on wrong side of garment. Use glue stick to hold binding in place. Stitch binding to garment, as in step 3, page 103.

6) Slip piece of fusible web inside mitered folds on both sides of binding to secure corner folds. Fuse in place. This may not be necessary for narrow binding.

Crocheted Edges

Single crochet, a basic crocheting stitch, forms a firm, decorative finish on a garment edge. Two rows of single crochet look like a corded edging. Add more rows for a wider band or a picot edge. Test the technique on a fabric scrap to be sure the fabric weave or knitted texture allows easy insertion of a crochet hook. Use pearl cotton, crochet cotton, or narrow ribbon compatible with the weight, texture, and fiber content of the garment. Use a small crochet hook that penetrates fabric easily.

How to Crochet an Edging

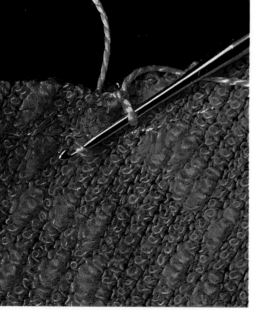

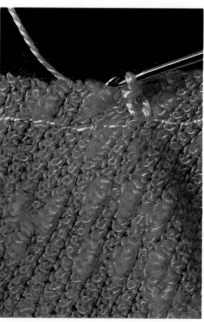

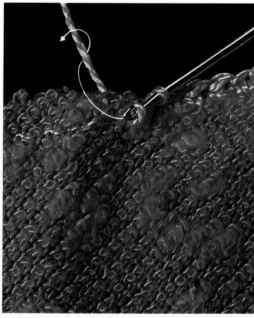

1) Staystitch garment on ⁵⁄₈" (1.5 cm) seamline; trim to ¼" (6 mm). Make slip knot on hook. From right side, insert hook through fabric. Wrap yarn over hook, and pull loop through to right side of garment. Two loops are now on hook.

2) Wrap yarn over hook and pull through both loops. One loop is left on crochet hook. This completes first single crochet stitch.

3) Work from right to left. Insert hook through fabric just below staystitching line to pull another loop through. Repeat single crochet across garment edge. Space stitches evenly so edge does not stretch or pull together.

Basic Crochet Stitches

Chainstitch. Make a slip knot on hook. Place yarn through left hand as shown. Wrap yarn over hook; pull yarn through loop on hook. This makes one chain. Repeat to add chains.

Slipstitch. With one loop on hook, insert hook through top of stitch. Wrap yarn over hook, and with one motion pull a loop through the stitch and the loop remaining on hook.

Single crochet. With one loop on hook, insert hook through top of stitch. Wrap yarn over hook, and pull up a second loop. Wrap yarn over hook. Pull through both loops. This completes a single crochet.

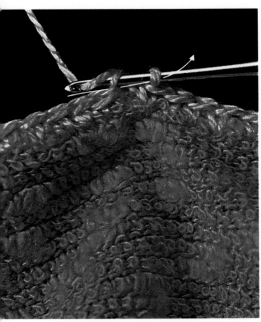

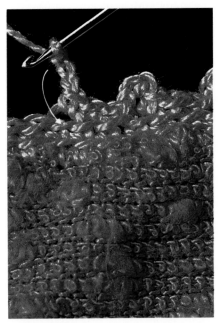

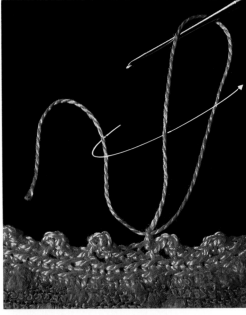

4) Slipstitch in first single crochet, with right side of garment facing you. (Do not turn work at end of neckline or sleeve edgings.) Make second row of single crochet on edge. Slipstitch at end. Finish off (step 6), or add picot edge.

5) Picot edge. On second row, single crochet in first three stitches; chain three, slipstitch in same stitch as last single crochet. Repeat pattern of single crochet and chainstitch around entire edge. Slipstitch to join stitches at end.

6) Finish by cutting off yarn, leaving about 6" (15 cm). Wrap yarn over hook, and pull through last loop. Pull yarn end to tighten. Thread end in blunt needle, and weave it back through edge.

Lined Facings & Mock Bound Hems

As a distinctive detail, the facing of a garment may be lined to the edge with the interfacing. This designer method is actually a shortcut, because the facing edge is quickly and neatly finished as a result. Although fusible interfacing is shown below, the technique works equally well with sew-in interfacing.

Use a mock bound hem for an inconspicuous edge finish. This hem has the appearance of narrow binding in matching fabric but is actually made from the turned-under edge of the garment. It is a method that works well on lightweight knits.

How to Line a Facing with Interfacing

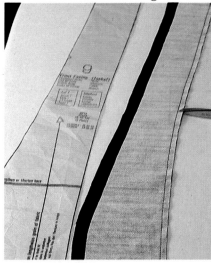

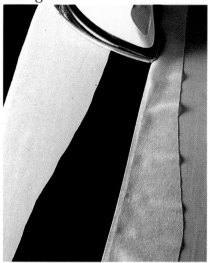

1) Stitch fusible interfacing to facing, right sides together, using ¼" (6 mm) seam allowance; nonadhesive side of interfacing is right side. Clip curves.

2) Press seam away from facing. To prevent interfacing from fusing to ironing board, be careful that the edge of the iron does not go beyond the seam allowance.

3) Fold interfacing on seamline. Finger-press fold, and position interfacing on wrong side of facing. Fuse interfacing to facing. Attach facing to garment.

How to Finish an Edge with a Mock Bound Hem

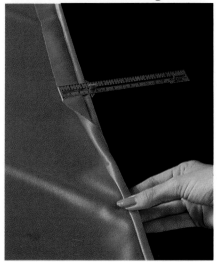

1) Fold up a 1¼" (3.2 cm) hem, right sides together; machine-stitch ¼" (6 mm) from fold. Wrap edge around to wrong side of garment, over stitching line.

2) Pin with raw edge covering stitching line. Shorten stitch length; stitch in the ditch from right side.

Alternative method: Fold edge under ¼" (6 mm). Adjust so depth from edge to fold is even all around and fold just meets stitching; pin. Slipstitch, working from wrong side and catching folded edge to stitching only.

Fringe

Making fringe requires little more than removing fabric yarns, one at a time, but it is a technique you can use in many creative ways. A simple fabric square with fringed edges can be worn as a shawl or scarf. Instead of hemming a skirt or overblouse, fringe the edge. Fringe strips of fabric for use as a separately applied trim; use fringed strips as seam insertions or decorative bindings. Fringe garment facings and sew them on the outside of a garment to decorate a neckline, patch pockets, or front closing.

Choose a plain-weave fabric for fringing. Loosely woven fabrics are ideal. Not only are the fabric yarns easy to remove, but the open look of fringe complements the fabric weave. If the fabric is woven from nubby or heavy yarns, the fringe will have an interesting texture. If the fabric is lightweight, the fringe will look delicate. On fabrics woven from more than one color of yarn, the colors of the fringe will be interesting variations of the fabric colors.

How to Fringe a Facing

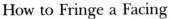

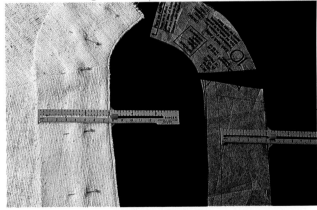

1) Cut facings, adding 1" (2.5 cm) to unnotched edges; join facing pieces. Stitch *right* side of facing to *wrong* side of garment. Press; trim and grade seam. Turn facing to right side of garment. Edgestitch.

2) Stitch through facing and garment at desired depth of fringe. Use short stitches to stabilize the fabric edge and prevent raveling after fringing.

3) Remove fabric yarns, beginning at edge. As you approach stitching, use blunt end of needle to pull yarns evenly toward edge of fringe.

4) Trim fringe along curves, using stitching as guideline to keep fringe even.

Piping

Purchased piping has one raised, decorative edge that can be inserted in a faced edge or seamline. The flat portion serves as the seam allowance and is positioned on the inside of the garment. The decorative piping edge may be corded for a rounded effect, scalloped like a picot edging, or braided.

Decorative piping is available in a variety of styles, such as those shown above. For dressy wear, use **(a)** braided cord or **(b)** metallic piping. For jackets and coats, use **(c)** piping or bias strips in the seam that joins the facing and lining. Choose **(d)** satin piping with metallic thread for an elegant look. Piping of **(e)** leather, **(f)** suede, and **(g)** jute give garments a sporty or classic look.

How to Insert Piping

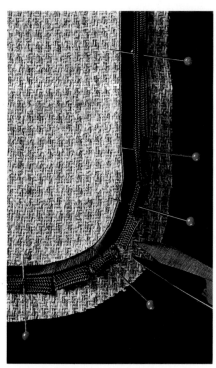

1) Pin piping to right side of garment, matching seamlines. Piped edge is toward center of garment section, and flat side is in seam allowance. Clip piping seam allowance so it lies flat at corners.

2) Clip piping seam allowance several times on curves.

3) Lap ends if piping does not end in a seam. Swing ends of piping into garment seam allowance. Trim and grade ends after stitching.

4) Baste piping to garment, using zipper foot. Stitch close to decorative edge of piping without crowding against raised edge.

5) Finish faced edge by stitching with garment side up so baste-stitching provides clear sewing guide. Using zipper foot, crowd stitches against piping.

6) Press seam to one side. Turn garment right side out. Piping makes a fine detail for jackets and coats because it stabilizes and strengthens the edge.

Decorative Seams

Ordinary seams become decorative details when you sew them inside out. This technique displays the stitches, and in some cases the seam allowances, on the outside of a garment. The result is a sophisticated self-trim.

Some of the seams shown here can be made only on an overlock sewing machine. However, you can achieve a similar look on a conventional zigzag sewing machine by combining straight and zigzag stitching or closely spaced decorative stitches.

Experiment with these seams for designer sewing. You can make an entire garment by selecting one of the seams, or mix several kinds of unusual seams within a single garment. You can also sew one or two accent seams in a garment, and sew the remaining seams in the regular manner. The knit shirt above uses a flat overlocked seam stitched with buttonhole/topstitching thread.

Further variations come from your choice of thread. Thread color can match or contrast with the garment fabric. Metallic threads and buttonhole/topstitching thread can be used. When working on an overlock machine, use novel materials such as pearl cotton, fingering yarn, or narrow ribbon to sew seams.

Types of Decorative Seams

Flat overlocked seam looks like seam used on baby's undershirt. Trellised stitches show on right side of garment for casual, sporty look. Method is often used on lightweight knits and sweatshirt fleece.

Reverse bound seam looks like decorative tuck on right side. Tuck shows wrong side of fabric that is normally hidden inside garment as seam allowance. This sewing method works best on straight seams and is especially suitable for knits.

Reverse plain seam shows off wrong side of fabric for interesting textural contrast. It is one way to handle seams on double-faced and reversible fabrics, as well as knits and other nonraveling fabrics. Use on straight or nearly straight seams.

Raised overlocked seam is ordinary three-thread overlocked seam sewn with wrong sides of fabric together. This technique suits all shapes of seams and any fabric, from delicate silks and sheers to sturdy denim and T-shirt knits.

How to Sew a Flat Overlocked Seam

1) Stitch seam, wrong sides of fabric together, with overlock machine set for 2-thread sewing. Adjust tension so needle thread loops at edge of fabric.

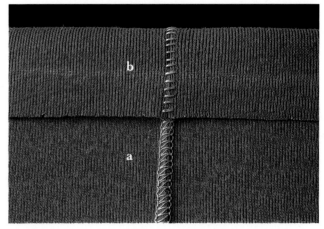

2) Open seam gently so raw edges lie flat. Press. Trellised stitches **(a)** show on right side, and ladder of stitches **(b)** shows on wrong side.

How to Sew a Reverse Bound Seam

1) Lap wrong side of one garment section over right side of adjoining section on seamlines. Stitch on seamline with straight stitch.

2) Fold seam allowance on right side under so that raw edge covers stitching line. Zigzag raw edge with short, narrow stitch, creating narrow tuck.

How to Sew a Reverse Plain Seam

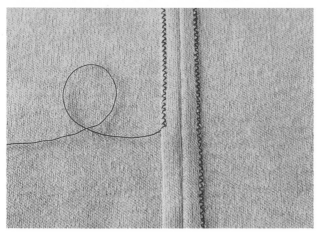

Stitch plain seam, wrong sides of fabric together. Press seam open. Trim both seam allowances to ¼" (6 mm). Stitch raw edge of each seam allowance to garment, using short, narrow zigzag stitches.

How to Sew a Raised Overlock Seam

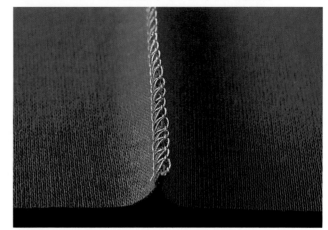

Stitch overlocked seam with wrong sides of fabric together. Press all seams in the same direction. Use buttonhole/topstitching thread for decorative seam on right side of garment.

Unique Embellishments

To create garments with a custom-made look, use decorative techniques that add color and texture. The choice of trimmings and decorative materials, as well as the choice of garment fabric and pattern style, will help determine the fashion statement that the garment makes. Sometimes it is the unusual position of the trim or embellishment that gives the garment a unique look.

Appliqué is a technique that is almost unlimited in the ways it can be used. Besides fabric, consider using ribbons or lace for appliqués. You can also use ribbon or yarn to weave a design along the border of a garment. Lace insertion is another technique for a border design. Cutwork is a technique that results in a lacy, embroidered look. Topstitching adds texture and can add color, too, if you use contrasting thread. Glittering trims such as sequins and beads also add texture, as well as sparkle or color, to a garment.

These details are easy to add because they require no changes in a pattern and no exotic construction methods. However, plan for these embellishments ahead of time. Most of them are easier to apply to flat garment sections or to the fabric before cutting out the pattern.

Appliqué by Machine

Appliqué is a method of decorating garments by sewing fabric cutouts to a background fabric. It is a good way to use a scrap collection, because small pieces of fabric are usually all you need for appliqués. Cut your own free-form shapes to design appliqués. Another simple approach is to cut an individual motif from a printed fabric for the appliqué. Designers use this method to create a custom look for ensembles made of separates.

Although almost any fabric can be appliquéd to another, machine techniques work best on light and mediumweight fabrics with a fine weave or knit. Because these techniques also require the use of

fusible interfacing, avoid using sheer, delicate, or open-weave fabrics. Naturally, the care requirements of appliqué fabrics should be compatible with the background fabric used for the garment.

In machine appliqué the fabric cutout is outlined with a satin stitch. Practice this stitch around corners and curves to get a feeling for handling the work. Use a special-purpose foot instead of a regular presser foot. Also use a quality sewing thread. For the least noticeable outline, match the thread to the appliqué. To accent the satin stitching, use metallic thread or a color of thread that contrasts with the garment and the appliqué.

How to Appliqué by Machine

1) **Back** appliqué fabric with lightweight fusible interfacing to prevent raveling. Cut appliqué from interfaced fabric. No seam allowances are needed around edge of appliqué. On delicate fabric, use weights instead of pins to hold pattern in place.

2) **Position** appliqué in place on garment section, using spray-on adhesive or glue stick as a temporary bond. When using spray-on adhesive, place appliqué upside down on paper before spraying.

3) **Stitch** appliqué in place with narrow zigzag stitch. For easier handling at the machine, finish appliqué before constructing garment.

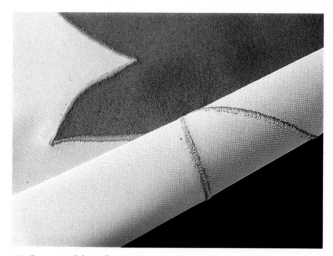

4) **Set** machine for satin stitch (short, wide zigzag). Position appliqué edge near the right of needle swing so stitches just cover raw edge.

Tips for Appliquéing

Stabilize appliqué area with special backing fabric; use nonwoven tear-away fabric designed especially for backing appliqués. This makes corners, points, and curves easier to handle on lightweight or stretchy background fabrics.

Turn outside corners by stitching off the appliqué a distance equal to half the width of satin stitching. Raise presser foot, pivot work to turn corner, and resume stitching. (Presser foot has been removed to show pivot point.)

Turn inside corners by stitching past corner a distance equal to half the width of satin stitching. Raise presser foot, pivot work to turn corner, and resume stitching. (Presser foot has been removed to show pivot point.)

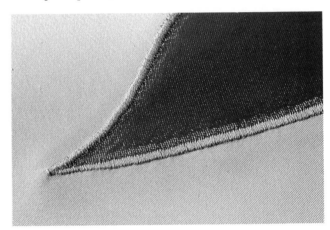

Turn points by gradually decreasing stitch width near tip. Stitch past appliqué, and pivot work. Gradually increase stitch width back to satin stitch as you sew away from tip.

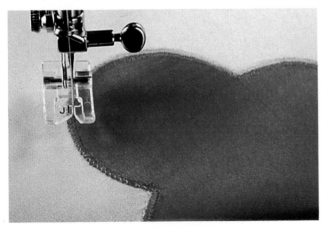

Round curves by pivoting work frequently to prevent gaps in stitching. Pivot with needle on outside of curve (appliqué side or garment side) for smooth satin-stitched outline.

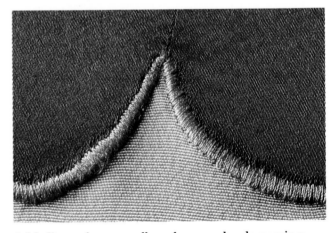

Add dimension to scalloped curves by decreasing stitch width as you stitch toward inner point. Pivot at point, and increase stitch width as you stitch away from inner point.

Lace Insertions

Lace is easy to work with for unique decorative treatments. It has a sheer net background that does not ravel, so you can sometimes eliminate extra finishing steps. Laces can be layered like a collage for bodice trims or skirt borders. With creative planning when you lay out a pattern on lace fabric, you can use a galloon border as prefinished skirt and sleeve hems.

The sheer insertion featured at right shows another way to use lace. The method preserves the transparent, open quality of lace. It looks attractive on fabrics such as crepe, lingerie tricot, satin, and handkerchief linen and works best on solid colors. You can also use this technique for applying individual lace motifs.

How to Sew a Lace Insertion

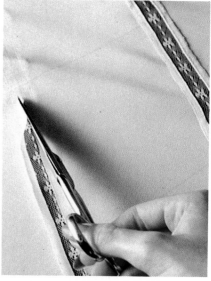

1) Position lace on right side of garment. Use pins, hand basting, or glue stick to hold in place. Lace insertion is easier to sew when garment section is flat, before seams have been sewn.

2) Edgestitch lace to garment. Use short straight stitch or short, narrow zigzag stitch. Match bobbin thread to garment, and needle thread to color of lace. Press from wrong side to blend stitches.

3) Trim away garment fabric ¼" (6 mm) from edgestitching, from wrong side. Use small, sharp scissors for careful trimming. Press edges back, and stitch close to folded edge.

Ribbon Appliqué

Ribbons are perfect for easy machine appliqué because they have prefinished edges. They are available in a number of fabrics, including satin, grosgrain, velvet, and novelty weaves. For an attractive border design, arrange several widths of matching ribbon in graduated rows with the widest size on the bottom. For a decorative effect, narrow ribbons can be applied to outline just the garment details, such as collar, cuffs, and waistband. A selection of different ribbons, varying in color, width, and texture, can be used to make an appliquéd lattice or an appliquéd plaid, as shown below. Use this technique just for details or for entire garment sections, such as yokes and sleeves.

How to Appliqué Ribbon

1) Arrange ribbon in desired design on garment section. Plan design so ribbons match at garment seams. Use glue stick or dissolving basting tape to hold ribbon in place.

2) Edgestitch ribbon, using straight stitch. Match needle thread to ribbon, and bobbin thread to background fabric. Where ribbons cross, stitch up to overlapping ribbon; skip overlap, and resume stitching on other side.

3) Clip threads, and pull the ends through to wrong side. If thread ends are too short to tie, apply liquid fray preventer to keep threads from pulling out.

Ribbon or Yarn Weaving

If you are working with a loosely woven or open weave fabric, weave ribbons in and out of the fabric to create an attractive border design. Use narrow ribbon and a blunt tapestry needle with a large eye for this decorative application of a basic running stitch. Ribbons 1/16", 1/8", or 1/4" (2, 3, or 6 mm) wide are suitable for making this detail. Smooth satin ribbons are ideal, because they contrast with rough fabric textures.

Lay the ribbon on the garment to plan placement. Cut the ribbon to the total length of each row to be woven, allowing generous amount for slack and for finishing ends. Allow extra to tie bows. If weaving ribbon close to a hemline, weave before sewing the garment hem.

How to Weave Ribbon

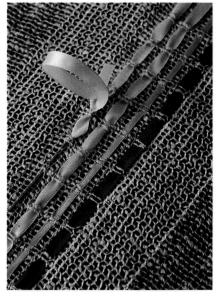

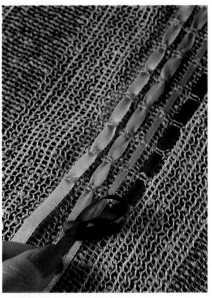

1) Thread tapestry needle with ribbon; make running stitches, leaving ribbon ends on outside if finishing with bow. Keep stitches equal by counting fabric threads between stitches. Allow enough slack so ribbon does not pull fabric. Keep ribbon flat, without twists.

2) Tie a bow or a knot on outside of the garment. Trim the streamers to desired length. If weaving several rows, tie bows after all the weaving is finished. They will be more uniform.

Alternative method: Pull ribbon ends to inside of garment to finish rows of weaving without bows. Stitch ribbon ends into seams; or knot ends, trim, and apply liquid fray preventer.

Cutwork by Machine

Cutwork is embroidery with portions of the design trimmed away; then the entire design is outlined in satin stitch. Cutwork has an open, delicate look similar to lace. It's a fine designer detail to add to a blouse or dress.

Commercial transfer patterns are available for cutwork embroidery; usually these are floral motifs. If you are developing your own cutwork design, be sure your plan includes bar-shaped bridges at frequent intervals; these not only connect cutout areas, but also stabilize the embroidery. Stencil patterns can also be used as cutwork designs because they include connecting bridges.

When embroidering cutwork by machine, you can maneuver the work easier if the design is fairly large and not too intricate. The design should also fit into an embroidery hoop. Then you can complete the cutwork without repeatedly changing the machine stitch settings.

Before cutting out the pattern piece, sew the cutwork on fabric large enough for moving the pattern around. This allows you to position the cutwork exactly where desired when laying out the pattern piece and saves wear and tear on the raw edges of the garment section.

For best results, select a closely woven background fabric that does not ravel easily, such as batiste, crepe, chambray, or lightweight linen. Two types of sewing thread are needed: regular all-purpose thread for the initial reinforcement stitches, and extra-fine or embroidery thread for the final satin stitches. Use size 11/75 machine needle with extra-fine thread. Also use a nonwoven tear-away fabric as a temporary backing to stabilize the entire design area for machine sewing.

How to Sew Cutwork by Machine

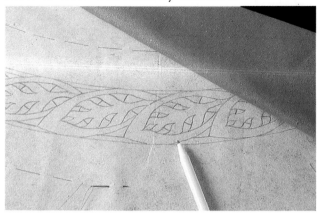

1) Mark cutwork design on nonwoven tear-away backing. Trace the pattern in reverse so it will be right side up on the right side of fabric. Baste tear-away backing on wrong side of fabric; backing should be larger than design area.

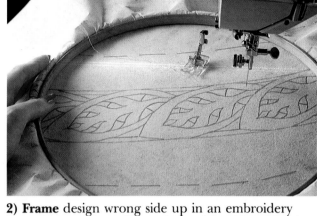

2) Frame design wrong side up in an embroidery hoop. Larger ring of hoop is on right side of fabric; smaller ring of hoop is on wrong side. Remove presser foot to position hoop under machine needle.

3) Reinforce edges of design with 3 rows of straight stitches on design lines. Use regular sewing thread and short stitch lengths, about 18 stitches per inch (2.5 cm). For better control, use special-purpose foot.

4) Cut away open areas of design close to reinforcement stitches, working with small areas at a time. Cut only through fabric; do not cut through tear-away backing; it remains to stabilize design area. Trim carefully with small, sharp scissors.

5) Satin stitch entire design from right side, beginning at center. (Reverse embroidery hoop so it is on right side of fabric.) Stitch small details and bars first, then outline. Use extra-fine or embroidery thread. Use narrow stitch wide enough to cover reinforcement stitches and catch raw edges of cutouts.

6) Remove tear-away backing carefully from wrong side of cutwork. In small areas, trim backing with small, sharp scissors rather than tearing it. Press cutwork from wrong side on padded surface.

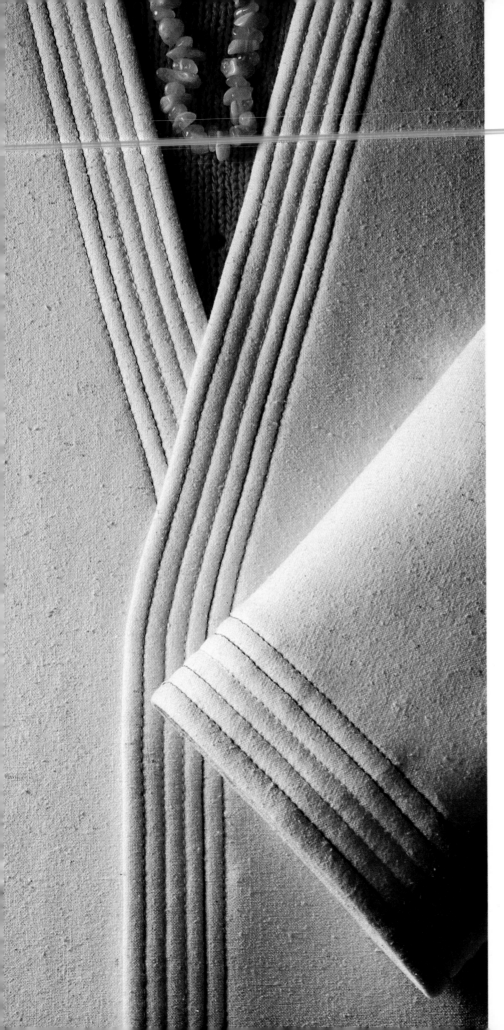

Topstitching

Topstitching is machine stitching that is meant to show on the right side of a garment. This classic detail is easy to master and keeps garment seams and edges crisp, neat, and flat.

Use one, two, or more rows of topstitching to accent seams and to outline garment edges such as the collar, cuffs, front closing, and hems. You can also cover a garment detail, such as a waistband or pocket flap, with closely spaced rows of topstitching. This creates a custom look that resembles trapunto quilting.

For best results, use a long machine stitch of about 8 to 10 stitches per inch (2.5 cm) and work from the right side of the garment. Topstitch with matching or contrasting thread or with buttonhole twist/topstitching thread. There are two types of twist. Silk twist should be used only on garments that will be drycleaned; polyester twist can be used on garments without restrictions for care. Because twist thread is heavier than all-purpose thread, use a large size 16/100 sewing machine needle or a special topstitching needle. Some sewing machines will sew with twist in the bobbin and the needle, but others may be more successful with regular sewing thread in the bobbin.

If the machine does not handle the twist in the upper tension, use twist in the bobbin only and topstitch from the wrong side of the garment. The fabric texture, bulk, and weight influence the result.

Tips for Topstitching

Test topstitching technique on fabric sample first. When topstitching a front closing, test on multi-layered sample with interfacing sandwiched inside. Topstitches should not sink into fabric; lengthen stitch and adjust needle thread tension until you are happy with the results.

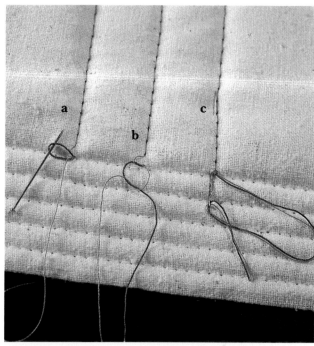

Secure topstitching by tying thread ends instead of backstitching. Backstitching spoils the look of topstitched details. Use a pin to pull the needle thread to the bobbin side **(a)**; tie a square knot **(b)**. Insert threads in hand sewing needle, and bury them invisibly between fabric layers **(c)**.

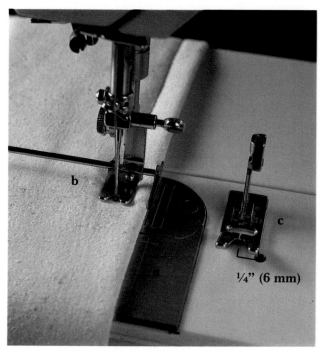

Space rows of topstitching evenly from edges and seams, and from each other, for professional look. When sewing near an edge, use markings on sewing machine needle plate **(a)** to position stitches. When topstitching seams or an area away from garment edge, use quilting foot **(b)** as guide. For ¼" (6 mm) wide measurement, use toe of presser foot **(c)**.

Use twin needle to topstitch two closely spaced rows with precision. This special needle accommodates two spools of thread and forms both rows of stitches from a single bobbin thread. Use twin-needle topstitching on collar, cuffs, hems and front placket opening of a shirt.

Glittering Trims

Beads and sequins make garments look glamorous for formal wear. Add these trims as one of the last steps in sewing a garment to better judge where to place the trim and how much to use. When trimming a lined garment, such as a jacket or cape, sew the trim before inserting the lining; the lining covers the stitches used to apply the trim.

Make the garment from a firm fabric, such as moire, velvet, or peau de soie, or a fabric with body, such as wool crepe or double knit, so the trim will not be too heavy for the fabric. You can also underline garment areas that will be trimmed, or back them with sheer fusible interfacing for additional support.

The key to putting metallic or jeweled trims on a garment is using a light touch. A few well-placed hand stitches will hold them in place. Press the trimmed garment with caution. Press from the wrong side, using a towel to pad the surface. Avoid pressing over trim; heat can damage beads and sequins.

Applying Glittering Trims

Sequins and beads add sparkle and opulence. They look best when applied to garments that have simple lines. When using trim to outline a shaped edge, such as a neckline, be sure the trim is flexible enough to ease smoothly around curves, or apply beads or sequins individually.

Tape band trims before cutting to prevent loss of sequins or beads as you plan trim placement on garment. Use a fine needle and matching thread or transparent nylon thread. To prevent tangling, use short length of thread and run it over beeswax.

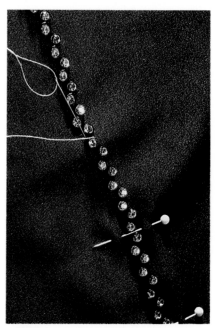

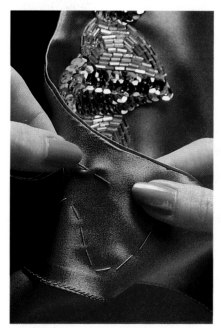

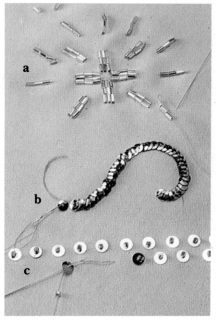

Work from outside of garment to apply pre-strung beads or sequins. Sew over string base of trim, placing one stitch between each segment, or at ¼" to ⅜" (6 mm to 1 cm) intervals.

Work from inside of garment to apply beaded or sequined band trims and appliqués. Sew through fabric base of trim with long running stitches. Allow enough slack in stitches so trim lies smoothly.

Attach individual beads, threaded several at one time, with running stitch (**a**). Attach sequins with a backstitch from hole to edge (**b**). Bring needle forward for next sequin, which will overlap first sequin and hide thread. Attach single sequins with a bead in center (**c**). Bring needle through hole, then through bead and back through hole.

Index